Shepherd's Balm

Monday Morning Calls
to the Shepherds of God's Flock

Richard Earl

©2010
Kalos Books
Cherry Hill, New Jersey

Dedication

To the pastor who toils joyfully in obscurity or wishes he/she could.

Thanks

To my family

My amazing wife, Faith, who believes in me and tells me the truth- faithfully.

Micah, Rachel and Rebekah who make me proud to be a father.

Mom and Dad who gave me more than I could have asked for.

Acknowledgments

His Thousand Hills Christian Retreat
Ed and Margie Hartman my mentors
Jess Bousa for believing
Tricia Purcell for caring
The flock at Mountainside Church

Published by Kalos Books, Cherry Hill, New Jersey.

Visit www.kalosbooks.com for more information on bulk discounts and special promotions, or email your questions to info@kalosbooks.com.

ISBN: 978-0-9846165-0-3

Cover Concept and Interior Design by Ron Kline

Printed in the United States of America

Contents

Shepherd's Balm

Monday Morning Calls
to the Shepherds of God's Flock

Richard Earl

Preface

Great is the need now and always for sources of encouragement, wisdom and challenge in the lives of those who give their all to caring for, teaching and leading the sheep otherwise known as the Church of Jesus Christ. I offer this small volume as a means for pastors to evaluate and meditate upon their work and lives, in light of our common experiences in ministry.

Shepherds have many responsibilities in caring for the sheep. It is their job to ensure their health, safety and welfare in what could be perilous circumstances. Among their tools are the shepherds staff, slingshot, and oil - used to anoint the heads of sheep to protect them from sunstroke. Earthly shepherds are in need of protection too, and that can only come from the Great Shepherd Himself, hence the title Shepherd's Balm.

The life of the present day pastor is filled with perils and opportunities, and they sometimes come dressed in the same clothes. Temptations, dangers, persecutions and conflicts can be, in retrospect, merely ways for God to shake us out of our present state and get us ready for one that is more productive. Surely he could keep us from these distressing experiences, but He does not. He seems oblivious to our plight when in reality He is making room for His grace to be sufficient, and for us to learn a new reliance upon Him, casting off old ways.

This volume is not meant to coddle or to soothe. It is not a bulwark against the forces we find within and without trying to tear us down. Rather, it is a dressing for our wounded and weary spirits to make us ready once again for the battle, the good fight of faith. The thoughts contained here are not naïve, but potent and time-tested, many coming from the old masters, and some from newly emerging voices.

The format of this book is quite simple. You will find an encouraging or challenging message about ministry followed by a verse of scripture and lines for journaling your reflections. You will also find images, brief quotes and exercises throughout the volume which are intended to provoke further thought and action.

The format reflects a deep respect for you and your ministry. I have limited reflective questions to just a few as I realize that you know how to make best use of this material in your own life. There is also plenty of room for freeform journaling if that is helpful to you.

It is my hope that this little volume will serve as a healing salve of sorts on Monday mornings, or at any time in the life of the shepherd. The individual entries are arranged in no real order, but have been given headings to distinguish the root issue addressed in each. There are 52 to provide balm for every Monday morning for a year with space provided for personal notes as the Lord speaks to you through these pages.

I have offered little comment to the devotional pieces, attempting to only offer words that hold weight, and hopefully speak for themselves. Some of the language is antiquated. If you struggle with a passage, stay at it, and you will learn its rhythms. I have discovered that the treasure is worth the mining.

You will notice that most of the authors assume the pastor is male. This can be attributed to their time in history. I have not corrected the language, but have not made an effort to exclude female ministers or ministry leaders. These pages speak to you as well as to your male counterparts.

Many of the authors contained in this volume are not widely known or read today. What I have discovered in reading their works is that while so much in our culture has changed, even more has remained the same in terms of shepherding God's people. People are still people, and just as we can see ourselves in the pages of ancient scripture, we can also find our likeness in the experiences of pastors whose work was done a century ago or more.

You may in a sense feel that certain entries found here have the effect of contradicting one another. This has to do with seeing things from both sides. For some of us, the weakness is severity, and so we must be encouraged to love our people more tenderly. Others are guilty of appeasing the flock, and need to be exhorted to more prophetic boldness.

This volume contains messages for God's ministers from many voices and from many ages. It has been my joy to collect their works over the past 25 years. It is my hope that, although some of these works I have drawn from are out of print and out of "style", you will search them out further and dig more deeply into the caverns of their wisdom. Most of what you find here could not be found with a Google search. You can't Google everything!

I recently made a new friend who pastors a church in Michigan. He formerly worked for a large Christian used bookseller where he would wander through their attic warehouse on breaks and rummage through the boxes full of treasure. On one such foray he was amazed to discover several boxes of three ring binders full of sermons diligently typed out single spaced and covered with copious handwritten notes in the margins. He looked for the name of the author everywhere, but never found it. He recently was able to obtain the binders as the inventory of the warehouse was sold. He continues his search to find the anonymous pastor. This book is written for that shepherd and millions of others like him who will never have their work published except in the hearts of their people. This is for the shepherd who toils in obscurity with his or her hands faithfully on the plow, and not looking back. Godspeed!

*"He who runs from God in the morning
will scarcely find Him the rest of the day."*
— *John Bunyan*

Great Reward

A minister, who does his work with an eye single to God's glory, leaving everything else behind, receives the best things the world affords. A multitude of people become his relatives and friends. Fathers and mothers are as proud of him as though he were a member of their family. Old men look on him lovingly as on a son. Young men look up to him reverently as to a father. Men of his own age love him as a brother. A large circle feels that in him they have a comrade and friend. He enjoys free access to many homes, houses and lands are his, not by legal title but by spiritual prescription. Appreciation, gratitude, affection, these are the gold, frankincense, and myrrh constantly poured out before him. If love is the best thing in the world, then the faithful pastor gets more of the Earth's richest treasure than any other man.

To be sure, he will not be loved by everybody. Jesus was careful to state that the good things would be accompanied by tribulations. These also are part of the minister's reward. The Pharisees and Sadducees and scribes will always be against him. Men not bad of heart, but of stupid ear will misunderstand him and misrepresent him. The idler will gossip about him and the ungrateful will return evil for good. Those possessed of demons will openly attack him. All this is to be expected. Is the pupil to be above his teacher, and the servant above his master? Think it not strange, young man, when this fiery experience overtakes you. Do not be thrown into panic because all men do not speak well of you. Do not cry and sob when you meet with opposition in your parish. Do your duty and you will stir up trouble, but you will never be left without faithful hearts to love you. When you go into Gethsemane, friends will remain praying at the gate, and if you die on the cross you will carry into heaven with you the affectionate devotion of many loyal hearts. There is nothing more beautiful on this earth than the love of a parish for a faithful pastor.

– Charles Edward Jefferson, *The Minister as Shepherd*, pp. 180-182

> *Surely goodness and mercy shall follow me*
> *all the days of my life.*
> *– Psalms 23:6 (NKJV)*

EXERCISE

Take time right now to thank the Lord for the privilege of serving him in ministry. Recall times when you complained of the way being hard and ask the Lord's forgiveness.

"If we think we are undervalued, let us weigh ourselves in God's balances, and we shall easily bear the slight."

– *RC Chapman*

Journal

Busy

The one piece of mail certain to go unread into my wastebasket is a letter addressed to the "busy pastor." Not that the phrase doesn't describe me at times, but I refuse to give my attention to someone who encourages what is worst in me. I'm not arguing the accuracy of the adjective; I am, though, contesting the way it's used to flatter and express sympathy.

"The poor man," we say. He's so devoted to his flock; the work is endless, and he sacrifices himself so unstintingly. But the word "busy" is the symptom not of commitment but of betrayal. It is not devotion but defection. The adjective busy set as a modifier to pastor should sound to our ears like adulterous to characterize a wife or embezzling to describe the banker. It is an outrageous scandal, a blasphemous affront.

I become busy for two reasons; both are ignoble: I am busy because I am vain. I want to appear important. Significant. What better way than to be busy? The incredible hours, the crowded schedule, and the heavy demands on my time are proof to myself — and to all who will notice — that I am important. If I go into a doctor's office and find there's no one waiting, and I see through a half-open door the doctor reading a book, I wonder if he's any good. A good doctor will have people lined up waiting to see him; a good doctor will not have time to read a book. Although I grumble about waiting my turn in the busy doctor's office, I'm also impressed with his importance.

Such experiences affect me. I live in a society in which crowded schedules and harassed conditions are evidence of importance so I develop a crowded schedule and harassed conditions. When others notice, they acknowledge my significance, and my vanity is fed.

I am busy because I am lazy. I indolently let others decide what I will do instead of resolutely deciding myself. I let people who do not understand the work of the pastor write the agenda for my day's work because I am too slipshod to write it myself. The pastor is a shadow figure in these people's minds, a marginal person vaguely connected with matters of God and goodwill. Anything remotely religious or somehow well-intentioned can be properly assigned to the pastor.

It was a favorite theme of CS Lewis that only lazy people work hard by lazily abdicating the essential work of deciding and directing, establishing values and setting goals, other people do it for us; then we find ourselves frantically, at the last minute, trying to satisfy a half dozen different demands on our time, none of which is essential to our vocation, to stave off the disaster of disappointing someone.

But if I vainly crowd my day with conspicuous activity or let others fill my day with imperious demands, I don't have time to do my proper work, the work to which I have been called. How can I lead people into the quiet place beside the still waters if I am in perpetual motion? How can I persuade a person to live by faith and not by works if I had to juggle my schedule constantly to make everything fit into place?

...The trick, of course, is to get to the calendar before anyone else does. I mark out times for prayer, for reading, for leisure, for the silence and solitude out of which creative work – prayer, preaching, and listening – can issue.

– Eugene Peterson, _The Contemplative Pastor_,
pp.17-23

_While it was still night, way before dawn, he got up
and went out to a secluded spot and prayed._
        – Mark 1:35 (The Message)

EXERCISE

Practice slowing. Look for opportunities to disrupt your need to get things done now. Take time to just be more relaxed with a less hurried agenda. Drive to work in the slow lane. If you go to the store, get in the longest line.

"Stars may be seen from the bottom of a deep well when they cannot be discerned from the top of a mountain."

– *CH Spurgeon*

Journal

3

Quenched

*I*t has been said that a good teacher will make the complex seem simple. This is the task of the pastor when he is in teaching mode. Making the Word and ways of God understandable is one of the joys of ministry. CW Slemming describes that process here.

Having reached the mountaintop the sheep are hot and thirsty. It may be that there is water in abundance gushing from a rock, or bounding over rocks and making its way swiftly down the side of a mountain: but this would not meet the need of the sheep, they could perish from thirst while water is abundant because they cannot drink from fast running water. It becomes necessary for the Shepherd to find a hollowed rock or something that will hold water and then he will bail it from the rich running stream into the receptacle or, if it be gushing from a rock with his staff he will scratch a channel in the earth from the water for a little distance and, following the earth the water will trickle along the channel, fill up the hollow, and so he has made a pool of still waters. From this, and others that he will make, the sheep drink.

Christ's love is like torrential waters. His grace is like a swelling tide. Who can approach the height and depth, length and breadth of the love of God? It passes understanding; it is beyond our comprehension, but from it comes that life-giving stream from which you and I find refreshment. God's Word, too, is like a great torrent. The depths of its mysteries will never be fathomed, the height of its glory never attained, the vastness of its wonders never discovered. It is a mine never to be exhausted, a spring never to run dry. It is the unsearchable riches of his grace but, while it remains beyond all human comprehension, we thank God for the still waters of that word to which we have been led and of which we have partaken, and we shall anticipate the day when we shall be able to eat of the hidden manna and drink of the fountainhead.

– CW Slemming, *Echoes from the Hills of Bethlehem*, pp.39-40

God, my shepherd! I don't need a thing. You have bedded me down in lush meadows, you find me quiet pools to drink from.
–*Psalm 23:1-2 (The Message)*

EXERCISE

This week explain the trinity to a child, the virtue of humility to a proud soul or the purpose of the cross to one who thinks they already know.

"The scarcest article today is plain faithfulness.
'Good and faithful servants' are at a premium."
– *Vance Havner*

Journal

4

No Straight Lines on Earth

I searched one day but could not find any straight lines on earth. Among the animals, the trees, the flowers, the multitudes of fish, and birds, even people, I searched in vain for anything that was purely aligned.

I found plenty of things that were pretty straight. Mighty redwoods, the edge of a bird's wing, mountain ridges, even flower stems and blades of grass. But none of them were completely straight. None of them qualified in my eyes.

I wondered and then realized that this is as it should be. God alone is completely straight. His creation, especially considering the Fall, is filled with anomalies and imperfections. We have knots in trees, bumpy noses, jagged seashores. Our ways are crooked, His way is straight. But there was more.

Sitting on the rocks of a jetty on my native Long Island's south shore one day I discovered not one, but two straight lines in the seascape before me.

They remain the only two straight lines I have ever noticed in the natural realm, though neither is actually located on terra firma itself.

First I saw that the spot where the water met the sky was perfectly straight. The horizon, the unreachable, fabled place always in the distance, always just out of reach, was perfectly straight. I think God and His preferred future for us are there.

Then just a few moments later, as I was still taking in this truth of the horizon, I saw another straight line. In fact, I saw lots of them. Through the clouds, dozens of sunbeams came cascading down from heaven in perfectly straight lines that were miles long. There was no effort, they were just there. Our heavenly Father remains the only source of straightness in a crooked world. The beams did not start at the earth's crust and fly upward, but came downward to us from Him.

In ministry, we sometimes think it is our job to straighten out what is crooked. Clearly this is an impossible task, and I don't think God ever called us to that. How many a minister has collapsed in exhaustion trying to weed out every trace of sin and corruption in the flock or in society?

Moses himself ministered to a mixed group of people. There were many sincere followers of God in the group to be sure, but there were also some real laggards. Imagine if Moses had spent his time trying to straighten them all out!

Our task is no different. For the sake of our sanity a balance must be struck between the discipline we bring as God's undershepherds and allowing the Lord to bring His own discipline. They are His sheep, not ours.

– Richard Earl

> _Now the mixed multitude who were among them_
> _yielded to intense craving; so the children of Israel also_
> _wept again and said: "Who will give us meat to eat?"_
> _–Numbers 11:4 (NKJV)_

EXERCISE

Take a piece of paper and write down the names of three EGRs in your sphere of influence (Extra Grace Required). Ask the Lord to show you how you can minister life to them. Be willing to offer encouragement, empathy, instruction, exhortation, admonition or even rebuke.

Journal

5

Among Stupid Souls

What are we to do when we come across stupid souls? Ignorant souls we can deal with, they need knowledge; the stupid soul does not need knowledge; the stupid soul needs to have the word of God until he is worried by it. The difficulty is how the worker is to get the word of God into its right place. Jesus Christ says the stupid soul is the one that "hears the word but does not understand it." "When anyone hears the word of the kingdom, and does not understand it, then the wicked one comes and snatches away what was sown in his heart…" (Matthew 13:19).

Does God hold a man culpable for being stupid spiritually? He certainly does. Every case of stupidity recorded in the Bible is punished by God. How can I get the word of God into a stupid soul?

Read 1 Samuel 15, and see how Samuel dealt with Saul. It's the commandment of God, "why did you not obey that?" Take the apostle Paul, the very same thing: "Oh foolish Galatians who hath bewitched you, that ye should not obey the truth?" And our Lord's own words: "Oh foolish man, and slow of heart to believe after all that the prophets have spoken!"

This is the time, Christian worker when you must use the word until you get it wedged in somehow in that stupid soul, until it rankles and worries its way to the soul's salvation or destruction, and there was never a class that will drive a worker closer to God than the stupid soul, they will tax every bit of patience and endurance you have. They always pretend to want to do something – "ever learning, and never able to come to the knowledge of the truth" – why? They would not obey the word they heard, that is the beginning.

You remember Samuel asked Saul if he had fulfilled the word of God with regard to the Amalekites, and Saul said he had: "Blessed be thou the Lord: I have performed the commandment of the Lord." And Samuel said, "What meaneth then this bleating of the sheep in my ears, and the lowing of the oxen which I hear?" It's pretending that is the first characteristic of the stupid soul.

When God gives you a word for a soul who is stupid, keep at it. This is the time when you have to keep using the verse God gives you for a soul: every time you meet him, every time you write to him, every time you talk to him. The only way you will stir up that one out of his stupidity is by driving home the word of God, and presently you will see that stupid soul saved from perdition, if it has not gone as far away from God as Saul, and as far away as many a stupid soul will go for lack of faithful workers.

When the Word of God has begun its piercing even to the dividing of soul and spirit, it will have its wonder-working way and heal and re-create and dissipate the stupidity.

– Oswald Chambers, *Workmen of God*, pp. 71-79

Then Jesus answered and said, "O faithless and perverse generation, how long shall I be with you? How long shall I bear with you? Bring him here to Me."
– Matthew 17:17 (NKJV)

EXERCISE

Practice coaching and active listening. It is sometimes hard for pastors to listen as much as we should. We are always called upon for advice and many people would rather be told what to do than to figure it out for themselves.

Journal

6

Ministry
in an Obscure Place

"The overwhelming majority of the Lord's workers labor anonymously in His vineyard-often in lonely places." (George Wood)

"One hundred years from now, it won't matter whether you drive an expensive or cheap car, whether you live in a mansion or a rented room, or whether you buy your clothes from Nordstrom's or Goodwill. It will not matter whether you pastored a large church or a small one; whether you preached to thousands or a handful; whether you had a public platform or ministered individually as a chaplain or counselor. What will matter 100 years from now is the legacy of your life that you pass on to others." (George Wood)

There is much that the Lord's true servants do which no human eye takes knowledge of. What they do they are to do as to the Lord, and to look for reward from him; learning also to have fellowship with Christ in his sufferings and service.

It is our wisdom not to seek praise of men. If, in our relationships with saints, rather than look after a good name, we seek to approve ourselves to God, a good name will surely follow us.

Look not at the quantity, but the quality of your service, whatsoever that service may be. It could be preaching, preaching is not the first thing: the heart must first be kept; then two or three words spoken in the power of the spirit may avail more than many a long discourse. (RC Chapman)

We all want to be noticed. This can even become an obsession. We strive, and seek some visible success so that we can point to it and receive the "atta boy" or pat on the back. This is especially true in our late 20s and through our 30s. We are affirmed by these things - numerical growth, recognition by our peers or a mentor, being noticed by society in general. When we don't receive them, we can feel empty.

Ideally, we ought to get these things from God. We ought not to crave the recognition of others. That is true, but we also need to know that we are making a difference, that our life's work matters.

A counterintuitive response is to seek ministry in an obscure place, not as a stepping stone, but as a life's work. The fact is, most of our churches are not large. In fact, quite the opposite is true. Most are not in booming communities. They are in obscure places.

Jesus was from an obscure place, and seemed to love being there. Many great people toil in obscurity their whole lives and are not seen for what they are until long after their death. Are you content to live such a life if it is God's will for you? Or will you need to be noticed and allow that to take you places the Lord does not send you?

– Richard Earl

With all this going for us, my dear, dear friends, stand your ground. And don't hold back. Throw yourselves into the work of the Master, confident that nothing you do for him is a waste of time or effort.
– 1 Corinthians 15:58 (The Message)

EXERCISE

Take time today to thank God for your place of ministry. He has chosen it for you, and designed you to minister to the people there. Name three blessings of being in that place.

Journal

7

For the Sheep

Mrs. Howard Taylor, in her life story of Pastor Hsi of North China, relates an incident which powerfully illustrates the sacrificial principle in a real pastor. Two Christian brothers named Chang had violently quarreled at one of the villages; and in a fit of rage the younger had thrown a cleaver at the elder brother's head. Fortunately it missed its mark, but struck an interested but unbelieving man by the name of Koh, wounding him severely in the knee. The whole community, Christian and heathen alike, were in a ferment.

Pastor Hsi was sent for. On his arrival, and it was bitterly cold wintry weather, he first of all amazed them by saying nothing, taking no refreshment after his journey, but seeking a place alone so he could pray. When he reappeared he made no attempt to address the disputants, or pacify the relatives of Koh, but made his way to where the wounded man was sitting, neglected in the general excitement, and asked to be allowed to do something for the suffering limb.

The effect was electric, and so changed the whole current of feeling a little by little Pastors Hsi was able to appeal to the disputants and diffuse the anger of the crowd. By associating himself as a Christian with the fault of the Changs he won the hearts of the heathen by his humility, and changed the disputants entirely, meanwhile presenting the true principles of Christianity. The climax was reached, however, when Hsi, realizing that something more was needed than words, deliberately went off to the nearest pawn shop, and came back without his fur-lined coat, thus being able to hand a substantial sum of money to the wounded man. This action broke everyone down entirely: they could not make up to him what he had sacrificed, and were compelled to see him start on the long journey home unprotected from the bitter weather. From that time the work flourished there in quite a special way. Another good Shepherd had sacrificed himself for the sheep.

It is these spiritual fathers who the assemblies need so much, and sadly lack in many places. Something more is required than "leaders"; something than "preachers"; something more than nominal figureheads: every flock of God needs fathering. A vital element is lacking where there is not personal care for individual souls, and an interest in them that is prepared to go to the point of sacrificing if need arise. We have rejoiced to meet such pastors here and there, and they are worth their weight in pure gold. Seldom do the assemblies themselves rightly value the true worth of such men; especially if they lack brilliant preaching gifts. Everyone runs after a good speaker. Perhaps this is another part of many a pastor's sacrifice. But if our Lord's parables count for anything they will not lose their reward on "that day."

– Donald Gee, _Concerning Shepherds and Sheepfolds_, pp. 3-6

For though you might have ten thousand instructors in Christ, yet you do not have many fathers; for in Christ Jesus I have begotten you through the gospel.
–_1 Corinthians 4:15 (NKJV)_

EXERCISE

Make a real effort this week to offer more questions than answers. Jesus did this. Push back against that drive to give the right answers and challenge others by asking questions to help them discover the answers themselves.

Journal

8

In Praise of Plodders

The climax of God's redeeming grace, according to Isaiah 40:31, is found in the strength which enables men to plod. To soar like an eagle is difficult, to run like a racehorse is more difficult still, but to walk and not faint – this is the greatest feat which the power of God can enable any man to do.

Shepherds neither fly nor run. A shepherd's work is prosaic, tedious, slow and obscure. Feeding sheep is his daily task and for this he needs neither the mettle of the racer nor the buoyancy of the eagle. He must have a genius for plodding. The clergyman who is able to trudge bravely through the years, filling the months with quiet honest work, pressing himself close upon his people and holding his people and himself close to the heart of Christ may cause little stir in the world but will make an impression which will be felt in heaven.

The farmer and preacher have need of the same patience, fidelity and pluck. The laws of the soil and the soul are inexorable and processes of growth in matter and spirit are orderly and slow. It must be hard plowing, faithful sowing, patient waiting, and skillful harvesting if the Lord of the harvest is to give a reward. A man who only prances or flies is a failure both in pulpit and field.

But this gift of plodding has not been given to all men. It is a form of genius, almost as invaluable and rare as that of the artist and poet. If a man does not possess it let them keep out of the ministry. He will be unhappy all his days and at eventide it shall be dark. The parish will be a cage against whose bars he will beat and bruise his impatient wings...repining always over imaginary races which he might have run and won.

Most of the best work done in the world is done by unnoticed toilers in obscure fields. Most of the best preaching is done in pulpits which have no halo around them in the public eye. The best sermons do not as a rule get into the papers, nor is any mention made of them by the reporters. The most influential preachers are not those most talked about but those whose words go deepest into the consciences and hearts of men. The church can afford a few eagles and racehorses of a nobler sort, but after all the solid and enduring work must be done largely by the plodders. My friend, if you're capable of walking without fainting, thank God and take courage. You are a person of gifts, and have in yourself indubitable evidence of the presence and favor of the Almighty. Others may astonish the nation by flying over every celebration, but at the end of the day you, having some precious seed, will come home rejoicing bringing your sheaves with you.

  – Charles Edward Jefferson, *Quiet Hints to Growing Preachers*, pp. 199-206

Do not neglect the gift that is in you, which was given to you by prophecy with the laying on of the hands of the eldership. Meditate on these things; give yourself entirely to them, that your progress may be evident to all.
  – 1 Timothy 4:14-15 (NKJV)

EXERCISE

Take time right now to thank the Lord for the privilege of serving him in ministry. Recall times when you complained of the way being hard and ask the Lord's forgiveness.

Journal

9

Tempted Fierce

Take heed to yourselves because you are exposed to greater temptations than others. If you will be the leaders against the Prince of darkness, he will spare you no further than God restrains him. He bears the greatest malice to those that are engaged to do him the greatest mischief. As he hates Christ more than any of us, because he is the general of the field, the captain of our salvation, and does more than all the world besides against his kingdom; so does he hate the leaders under him, more than the common soldiers: he knows what a rout he may make among them, if the leaders fall before their eyes. He has long tried that way of fighting, neither against great nor small comparatively, but of smiting the shepherds that he may scatter the flock; and so great has been his success this way, he will follow it as far as he is able.

Take heed therefore, brethren, for the enemy has a special eye upon you. You shall have his most subtle insinuations, and incessant solicitations, and violent assaults. As wise and learned as you all are, take heed to yourselves, lest he outwit you. The devil is a greater scholar than you, a more nimble disputant; he can transform himself into an angel of light to deceive; he will get within you, and trip up your heels before you are aware; he will play the juggler with you undiscerned, and cheat you of your faith or innocence, and you shall not know that you have lost it; nay, he will make you believe it is multiplied or increased when it is lost. You shall see neither hook nor line, much less the subtle angler himself, while he is offering you his bait. And his bait will be so fitted to your temper and disposition that he will be sure to find advantages within you, and make your own principles and inclinations betray you; and whenever he ruins you, he will make you the instrument of ruin to others.

Oh what conquests will he think he has gotten, if he can make a minister lazy and unfaithful – if he can tempt a minister into covetousness or scandal. He will glory against the church, and say, these are your holy preachers! He will glory against Christ himself, and say, these are thy champions? I can make your chief servants abuse you. I can make the stewards of your house unfaithful. If he did so insult God upon a false premise, and tell them you could make Job curse Him to His face, what will he do if he should prevail against us? At last he will exult as much over you, that he could draw you to be false to your great trust, and to blemish your holy profession, and to do so much service to him who was your enemy.

Oh do not so far gratify Satan – do not afford him so much sport: do not permit him to use you as the Philistines did Samson – first to deprive you of your strength, and then to put out your eyes, and so to make you the matter of his triumphant derision.

Take heed to yourselves, because there are many eyes upon you, and consequently there will be many to observe your falls.

– Richard Baxter, *The Reformed Pastor*, pp. 117-119

Take heed to yourself and to the doctrine. Continue in them, for in doing this you will save both yourself and those who hear you.
– 1 Timothy 4:16 (NKJV)

Thou wouldst not have thy man crushed back to clay;

It must be, God, thou hast a strength to give

To him that fain would do what thou dost say;

Else how shall any soul repentant live,

Old griefs and new fears hurrying on dismay?

Let pain be what thou wilt, kind and degree,

Only in pain calm thou my heart with thee.

– George MacDonald, *Diary of an Old Soul*, February 10

EXERCISE

Share a burden, struggle or temptation with a trusted ministry friend this week. Pray for one another for strength in the battle.

"When we confess our virtues we are competitors,
when we confess our sins we are brothers."
–Karl Barth

Journal

10

A Hungry Flock

Not living so near to God ourselves as we should, we are afraid to come near to the consciences of our people.

Some prefer popularity to plain dealing. We love to see a crowd of worldly-minded hearers rather than "a little flock, a peculiar people, zealous of good works." We dare not shake our congregation to purpose, lest our 5000 should, in three years time, be reduced to 120.

Luther's advice "so preach that those who do not fall out with their sins may fall out with thee," is more and more unfashionable. Under pretense of drawing our hearers by love, some of us softly rock the cradle of carnal security in which they sleep.

For "fear of grieving the dear children of God," we let "buyers and sellers, sheep and oxen," yea goats and lions fill the temple undisturbed. And because "the bread must not be kept from the hungry children," we let those who are wanton make shameful waste of it and even allowed dogs which we should "beware of" and noisy parrots that speak shibboleth to do the same.

We forget that God's children are led by the Spirit who is "the Comforter" Himself; that they are all afraid of being deceived, all "jealous for the Lord of hosts," and therefore prefer a preacher who "searches Jerusalem with candles" and cannot suffer God's house to be made a "den of thieves" to a workman who "whitewashes the noisome sepulchers".

– John Fletcher, A Message for Pastors, *Refiners Fire Journal* vol. 1, p. 119

EXERCISE

Pledge to yourself and to God to never compromise the Word in preaching for fear of any person or of offending the people. Prefer to offend them than to offend God.

Shepherd the flock of God which is among you, serving as overseers, not by compulsion but willingly, not for dishonest gain but eagerly; nor as being lords over those entrusted to you, but being examples to the flock; and when the Chief Shepherd appears, you will receive the crown of glory that does not fade away.
– 1 Peter 5:2-4 (NKJV)

"Necessitated by our pride, God takes us upward only by a downward path called humility."

—Richard Earl

Journal

11

Thoughts on Solitude

It takes 20 times more the amount of amphetamine to kill individual mice than it takes to kill them in groups. Experimenters also find that a mouse given no amphetamine at all will be dead within 10 minutes of being placed in the midst of a group on the drug. In groups they go off like popcorn or firecrackers. Western men and women especially, talk a great deal about being individuals. But conformity to social pattern is hardly less remarkable than that of the mice - and just as deadly!

In solitude we find the psychic distance, the perspective from which we can see, in the light of eternity, the created things that trap, worry, and oppress us. Thomas Merton writes:

"That is the only reason why I desire solitude – to be lost to all created things, to die to them and to the knowledge of them, for they remind me of my distance from You: that You are far from them, even though You are in them. You have made them and your presence sustains their being and they hide you from me."

But solitude, like all of the disciplines of the spirit, carries its risks. In solitude, we confront our own soul with its obscure forces and conflicts that escape our attention when we are interacting with others. Thus "solitude is a terrible trial, for it serves to crack open and burst apart the shell of our superficial securities. It opens out to us the unknown abyss that we all carry within us and discloses the fact that these abysses are haunted." We can only survive solitude if we cling to Christ there. And yet what we find of Him in that solitude enables us to return to society as free persons.

– Dallas Willard, *The Spirit of the Disciplines*, pp 160-161.

Indeed the hour is coming, yes, has now come, that you will be scattered, each to his own, and will leave Me alone. And yet I am not alone, because the Father is with Me.

– John 16:32 (NKJV)

And after he had dismissed the crowds, he went up on the mountain by himself to pray. When evening came, he was there alone.

–Matthew 14:23 (ESV)

EXERCISE

Practice solitude. Find a room at church, or a quiet spot where there are no people and simply be with God. Don't talk to Him, just be silent and alone before Him. Do this for at least 30 minutes.

Journal

12

Present in the Moment

I was on a personal retreat, and took a long walk one day in the bitter cold. The road was straight and level and the sky clear. Because of the straightness of the road and driven by the cold, I felt my steps oddly small. In the vastness of the cold Pennsylvania hills my stride seemed profoundly short and insignificant. It seemed like I would never get there, though I was going nowhere in particular.

I thought about lengthening my stride to speed things up. I am always so concerned with speed, but here I was on retreat and there was no need for haste. Speed for me is sometimes a virtue, but is often the cause of sloppy work and inattention to detail and the people I am with. The list of routine pastoral duties is often long, and getting through them quickly affords me more time for other things. But I sometimes regret my rapidity as it means I am not completely present in the moment. I want to be present in the moment and communicate to the people I am with that they are valued.

The reason for my walk was to commune singularly with my heavenly Father. That was the only reason. I do not like the cold, and I am not especially fond of lonely walks. I would much prefer to walk with my family or group of friends along a hot beach. But there I was determined to pour out my heart to God, and was hopeful of a response. I was with the King of the Universe who was bending His mighty ear to hear my every plea, and my chief concern was in getting it over with. How many a divine appointment has been missed in the name of efficiency?

– Richard Earl

And Jesus answered and said to her, "Martha, Martha, you are worried and troubled about many things. But one thing is needed, and Mary has chosen that good part, which will not be taken away from her."
–Luke 10:41-42 (NKJV)

EXERCISE

Visit a nursing home for no professional reason. Wear no clergy attire, do not introduce yourself as a pastor. Simply love the residents and staff as a volunteer helper.

"Our ways don't become His ways
until we are undone..."

— Terry Taylor

Journal

13

The Secret Fight

The battle is lost or won in the secret places of the will before God, never first in the external world. The Spirit of God apprehends me and I am obliged to get alone with God and fight the battle out before Him. Until this is done, I lose every time. The battle may take one minute or a year, that will depend on me, not on God; but it must be wrestled out alone before God, and I must resolutely go through the hell of a renunciation before Him. Nothing has any power over the man who has fought out the battle before God and won there.

If I say—"I will wait until I get into the circumstances and then put God to the test," I shall find I cannot. I must get the thing settled between myself and God in the secret places of my soul where no stranger intermeddles, and then I can go forth with the certainty that the battle is won. Lose it there, and calamity and disaster and upset are as sure as God's decree. The reason the battle is not won is because I try to win it in the external world first. Get alone with God, fight it out before Him. Settle the matter there once and for all.

– Oswald Chambers, *Called of God*

And He said, "Your name shall no longer be called Jacob, but Israel; for you have struggled with God and with men, and have prevailed."
        – *Genesis 32:28 (NKJV)*

EXERCISE

Identify the one thing in your life that you wish you could gain control of. Take some hours of personal retreat this week to wrestle it out before God. Fight to win.

"Some men's religion fails at the pinch: that of others does not appear to pluck up heart until the pinch comes."

– CS Lewis

Journal

14

God's Man

There are two extreme tendencies in the ministry. The one is to shut itself out from intercourse with the people. The monk, the hermit were illustrations of this; they shut themselves out from men to be more with God. They failed, of course. Our being with God is of use only as we expend its priceless benefits on men.

We shut ourselves to our study, we become students, bookworms, Bible worms, sermon makers, noted for literature, thought, and sermons; but the people and God, where are they? Out of heart, out of mind. Preachers who are great thinkers, great students must be the greatest of prayers, or else they will be the greatest of backsliders, heartless professionals, rationalistic, less than the least of preachers in God's estimate.

The other tendency is to thoroughly popularize the ministry. He is no longer God's man, but a man of affairs, of the people. He prays not, because his mission is to the people. If he can move the people, create an interest, a sensation in favor of religion, an interest in the work— he is satisfied. His personal relation to God is no factor in his work. Prayer has little or no place in his plans.

The disaster and ruin of such a ministry cannot be computed by earthly arithmetic. What the preacher is in prayer to God, for himself, for his people, so is his power for real good to men, so is his true fruitfulness, his true fidelity to God, to man, for time, for eternity.

It is impossible for the preacher to keep his spirit in harmony with the divine nature of his high calling without much prayer. That the preacher by dint of duty and laborious fidelity to the work and routine of the ministry can keep himself in trim and fitness is a serious mistake. Even sermon-making, incessant and taxing as an art, as a duty, as a work or as a pleasure, will engross and harden, will estrange the heart, by neglect of prayer, from God. The scientist loses God in nature. The preacher may lose God in his sermon.

– EM Bounds, *The Preacher and Prayer*, pp. 26-28

While it was still night, way before dawn, he got up and went out to a secluded spot and prayed.
—Mark 1:35 (The Message)

O Lord, I have been talking to the people;

Thought's wheels have round me whirled a fiery zone,

And the recoil of my words' airy ripple

My heart unheedful has puffed up and blown.

Therefore I cast myself before thee prone:

Lay cool hands on my burning brain, and press

From my weak heart the swelling emptiness.

– George MacDonald, *Diary of an Old Soul*,
January 31

EXERCISE

If you are an introvert and contemplative, make an effort this week to turn your heart and mind outward toward others. If you are an extrovert, make an effort to withdraw from the social situations and press into God.

Journal

15

Religious Shopkeepers

American pastors are abandoning their posts, left and right, and at an alarming rate. They're not leaving the churches and getting other jobs. Congregations still pay their salaries. Their names remain on the church stationery and they continue to appear in pulpits on Sundays. But they are abandoning their posts, their calling. They have gone whoring after other gods. What they do with their time under the guise of pastoral ministry hasn't the remotest connection with what the church's pastors have done for most of 20 centuries.

The pastors of America have metamorphosed into a company of shopkeepers, and the shops to keep are churches. They are preoccupied with shopkeepers concerns — how to keep customers happy, how to lure customers away from competitors down the street, how to package the goods so that the customers will lay out more money.

Some of them are very good shopkeepers. They attract a lot of customers, pulling great sums of money, develop splendid reputations. It is still shop keeping; religious shop keeping, to be sure, but shop keeping all the same. The marketing strategies of the fast food franchise occupy the weak minds of these entrepreneurs; while asleep they dream of the kind of success that will get the attention of journalists. "A walloping great congregation is fine, and fun," says Martin Thornton, "but what most communities really need is a couple of saints. The tragedy is that they may well be there in embryo, waiting to be discovered, waiting for sound training, waiting to be emancipated from the cult of the mediocre."

The biblical fact is that there are no successful churches. There are, instead, communities of sinners, gathered before God week after week in towns and villages all over the world. The Holy Spirit gathers them and does his work in them. In these communities of sinners, one of the sinners is called pastor and given a designated responsibility in the community. The pastor's responsibility is to keep the community attuned to God. It is this responsibility that is being abandoned in spades.

– Eugene Peterson, *Working the Angles*, pp. 1-2

Therefore I urge you to reaffirm your love to him.
       – 2 Corinthians 2:8 (NKJV)

EXERCISE

In what ways does your church resemble a vendor of religious goods and services? Begin a discussion this week with church leaders or local pastors by asking this question.

"The organized church has wrongly changed the emphasis from seed-sowing to tree growing."
— Herbert Lockyer

Journal

16

Killing the Heart

One-day grandma was in her backyard, polishing a large stone. It was a boulder that sat athwart her garden, too big to move. It was one of those stones round and smooth, tumbled by eons of wind and ice and water, deeply embedded with glittery chunks of mineral. She was polishing it with sandpaper. Her logic was that, since she couldn't be rid of the thing she may as well beautify it, try to remove the scumble of dullness on its surface and honed to a lustrous sheen. She was going to make it the centerpiece of her garden.

But she got more than that. As she sanded, she noticed a thin sifting of gold gathering on the stone. She pressed the moist tip of her finger into it and pulled up a caking of gold dust. Her heart raced. She sanded faster, leaning her whole body into it, and more gold appeared. Now she was scrubbing that rock as if it were a blood stain, with strong, sweeping strokes, bone and sinew bent to the work. Gold accumulated rapidly.

She caught the virus (gold fever) in one swoop. She understood with perfect instinct what all this time she dismissed as sheer nonsense: grown men squandering all else – homes and farms and families and reputations – and flinging themselves headlong into reckless escapades, spending their years burrowing beneath tree roots, grubbing through silt beds.

But now she had it too: gold fever. She was going to be rich.

She stopped a moment, to wipe her brow, to rest a spell. And that's when she noticed that something was wrong with her wedding ring. The topside was normal, but the underside, the part that nestled in the crease where her finger joined her palm, wasn't. The band there was thin as a cheese slicer wire, thin as a filament.

She had nearly sanded her wedding ring clean off. All that gold was merely filings. It was the remnants of her heirloom. It was her treasure reduced to dust. It was fool's gold.

I laughed the first time my wife told me that story, but only the first time. After that it may be sad. It's sad for its own sake, an aging woman giddy as a schoolgirl, heady with a sense of windfall, dreaming of a new dress and a real holiday, and the next moment crestfallen, stinging with shame over her coveting and naïveté.

But it's also sad because most of my own life I've repeated, again and again, grandma Alice's mistake. I squandered treasures in pursuit of dust. I've eroded precious, irreplaceable things in my efforts to extract something that's not actually there. I've imagined I'm on the trail of a groundbreaking discovery, only to find I'm at the tail end of a hard loss. Here are a few: all the times I never swam in a cool lake with my children, made a snowman or baked sugar cookies with them, lingered in bed with my wife on a Saturday morning, or helped a friend in need, all because I was in a hurry to – well, that's just it: I don't remember what. I was just in a hurry…

…Someone asked me recently what was my biggest regret in life. I thought a moment, surveying the vast and cluttered landscape of my blunders and losses, the evil I have done, evil that's been done against me.

"Being in a hurry," I said.

"Pardon?"

Being in a hurry. Getting to the next thing without fully entering the thing in front of me. I cannot think of a single advantage I've ever gained from being in a hurry. But a thousand broken and missed things, tens of thousands, lie in the wake of all that rushing.

Through all that haste, I thought I was making up time. It turns out I was throwing it away. Sanding away my wedding ring.

...The Chinese join two characters to form a single pictograph for busyness: heart and killing. That is stunningly incisive. The heart is the place the busy life exacts its steepest toll. Busyness kills the heart. Busyness makes us stop caring about the things we care about. And not only that, busyness also robs us of knowing God the way we might.

– Mark Buchanan, *The Rest of God*, pp. 43-48

Remember your Creator before the silver cord is loosed,
Or the golden bowl is broken, Or the pitcher shattered
at the fountain, Or the wheel broken at the well.
                          – Ecclesiastes 12:6 (NKJV)

EXERCISE

Take a walk today with your wife or child with no agenda, no errand to run, simply walk and be.

"*If you would win the world, melt it, do not hammer it.*"

—*Alexander MacLaren*

Journal

17

A Step in the Right Direction

I have found my time of greatest peril and temptation is not in the hour of deepest distress, but in the hour just after a great spiritual victory. It is then that our guard must be up, and we must position ourselves to fight, for the enemy knows we may be unprepared.

We must be careful as pastors not to excuse ourselves from the conviction of the Holy Spirit and working of repentance. We are just as prone to "go easy on ourselves" as anyone else. This word from JB Stoney should serve as a warning and reminder to us all.

When the conscience is in exercise, there is great need that it should not be checked or quieted by partial action, or by imperfect intelligence. The conscience of a saint is awakened by the spirit of God to seek relief from the presence of evil around. This is a true, healthy purpose, and most blessed if effectively carried out according to the word of God. The danger and consequent loss is when compromise is entered into, when the conscience is quieted by one step, rather than by a definite and clear escape from a place of grievance. And thus, alas! The flesh is spared and the spirit of God grieved, and there is really no progress.

This often occurs in our Christian history; the conscience has been aroused, but to meet it fully as in the light of God's presence would cost our nature too much. Of course we do not reason in this plain way with ourselves; but do we not often, perhaps years afterwards, discover that it was really sparing ourselves which led to our resisting the demands and strivings of our conscience? For now, being in the place of blessing which our conscience had long before indicated, we see how we had deceived ourselves, and thus had hindered our own blessing; and all because we feared the personal trial to which we should have been exposed in reaching it.

It is well to be warned of this device or weakness, from which all suffer many times and in many ways — one which I may call an effort to appease the conscience without putting the flesh to much sacrifice — because if we see how we have been deceived in this subtle way, we are the more careful to attend to our conscience, and how God is speaking to it, and how we may quiet it at the smallest cost to ourselves. In short, as a rule, when the conscience is arrested or exercised, the first thought is, not what will at all costs satisfy it according to God, but on the contrary, how I can answer its demand without involving myself in loss and pain.

Finally, if I make my own ease of mind or judgment the measure of my action, instead of the revealed will of God and the leading of the Holy Spirit, the consequence will be that it will be more difficult for me to be led on than for those who have not moved at all. For at the bottom the hindrance to me is the desire to spare myself the sacrifice; and according as I spare myself I deprive myself, in a hundredfold proportion, of the blessing contingent on faithfulness; and hence they who rest satisfied with the right step never advance in truth or knowledge beyond a certain point.

– JB Stoney, *The Refiner's Fire Journal*

But you, O man of God, flee these things and pursue righteousness, godliness, faith, love, patience, gentleness.

– 1 Timothy 6:11 (NKJV)

EXERCISE

Search your heart and mind for any areas of incomplete repentance or excusing of sin and determine to let God finish the work.

Journal

18

The Blind Eye
and the Deaf Ear

Having often said that a minister ought to have one blind eye and one deaf ear, I have excited the curiosity of several brethren, who have requested an explanation; for it appears to them, as it does also to me, that the keener eyes and ears we have the better. Well, gentlemen, since the text is somewhat mysterious, you shall have the exegesis of it.

A part of my meaning is expressed in plain language by Solomon, in the book of Ecclesiastes (7:21): "Also take no heed unto all words that are spoken; lest thou hear thy servant curse thee." The margin says, "Give not thy heart to all words that are spoken"—do not take them to heart or let them weigh with you, do not notice them, or act as if you heard them. You cannot stop people's tongues, and therefore the best thing is to stop your own ears and never mind what is spoken.

There is a world of idle chit-chat abroad, and he who takes note of it will have enough to do. He will find that even those who live with him are not always singing his praises, and that when he has displeased his most faithful servants they have, in the heat of the moment, spoken fierce words which it would be better for him not to have heard. Who has not, under temporary irritation, said that of another which he has afterwards regretted? It is the part of the generous to treat passionate words as if they had never been uttered. When a man is in an angry mood it is wise to walk away from him, and leave off strife before it be meddled with; and if we are compelled to hear hasty language, we must endeavour to obliterate it from the memory, and say with David, "But I, as a deaf man, heard not. I was as a man that heareth not, and in whose mouth are no reproofs." Tacitus describes a wise man as saying to one that railed at him, "You are lord of your tongue, but I am also master of my ears"—you may say what you please, but I will only hear what I choose.

We cannot shut our ears as we do our eyes, for we have no ear lids, and yet, it is, no doubt, possible to seal the portal of the ear so that nothing contraband shall enter. We would say of the general gossip of the village, and of the unadvised words of angry friends— do not hear them, or if you must hear them, do not lay them to heart, for you also have talked idly and angrily in your day, and would even now be in an awkward position if you were called to account for every word that you have spoken, even about your dearest friend.

...Know nothing of parties and cliques, but be the pastor of all the flock, and care for all alike. Blessed are the peacemakers, and one sure way of peacemaking is to let the fire of contention alone. Neither fan it, nor stir it, nor add fuel to it, but let it go out of itself. Begin your ministry with one blind eye and one deaf ear.

– Charles H Spurgeon, _Lectures to My Students_, Volume II Lecture IX

The discretion of a man makes him slow to anger, and his glory is to overlook a transgression.
– Proverbs 19:11 (NKJV)

EXERCISE

Look up an old adversary and give him a gift and/or take him to lunch.

Journal

19

Waiting on God

*The Lord upholdeth all that fall, and raiseth up all
those that be bowed down The eyes of all wait upon
thee; and thou givest them their meat in due season.*
                                                    —Psalm 145:14-15 (KJV)

If an army has been sent out to march into an
enemy's country, and tidings are received that
it is not advancing, the question is at once asked,
what may be the cause of delay. The answer will very
often be: "waiting for supplies". All the stores of
provisions or clothing or ammunition have not
arrived; without these they dare not proceed. It is no
different in the Christian life: day by day, at every
step, we need our supplies from above. And there is
nothing so needful as to cultivate that spirit of
dependence on God and of confidence in him which
refuses to go on without the needed supply of grace
and strength.

If the question be asked, whether this is any different from what we do when we pray, the answer is, that there may be much praying with very little waiting on God. In praying we are often occupied with ourselves, with our own needs... In waiting upon God, the first thought is of God upon whom we wait. We enter his presence, and feel we need just to be quiet, so that he, as God, can overshadow us with Himself. God longs to reveal Himself, to fill us with himself. Waiting on God gives him time in his own way and divine power to come to us...

When you pray, let there be intervals of silence, reverent stillness of soul, in which you yield yourself to God, in case He may have something he wishes to teach you or to work in you. Waiting on him will become the most blessed part of prayer, and the blessing thus obtained will be doubly precious as the fruit of such Fellowship with the Holy One.

The eyes of all wait upon Thee, and you give them their meat in due season. Dear soul, God provides in nature for the creatures he has made: how much more will He be providing grace for those he has redeemed. Learn to say of every want, and every failure, and every lack of needful grace: "I have waited too little upon God or he would have given me in due season all I needed." And say then too – "my soul wait thee only upon God."

– Andrew Murray, *Waiting on God*, pp. 29-32

*And He said, "My Presence will go with you, and I will
give you rest." Then he said to Him, "If Your Presence
does not go with us, do not bring us up from here."*
                                        – Exodus 33:14-15 (NKJV)

Come to me, Lord: I will not speculate how,

Nor think at which door I would have thee appear,

Nor put off calling till my floors be swept,

But cry, "Come, Lord, come any way, come now."

Doors, windows, I throw wide; my head I bow,

And sit like someone who so long has slept

That he knows nothing till his life draw near.

  – George MacDonald, *Diary of an Old Soul*,
    January 30

EXERCISE

Find yourself a quiet room and simply BE with
God for unspecified period of time. Practice waiting
on Him.

Journal

20

An Armored Saint

In an army called to active duty, weapons are frequently battered and broken. One man has his helmet broken, another his sword bent, a third his pistol broken. So replacements are often necessary. In one temptation you may have your helmet of hope crushed or your charity trampled upon. You need an armorers shop near at hand to make up for losses as quickly as possible, for Satan is most likely to attack when you are least prepared to repel his charge.

"Simon, Simon, Satan hath desired to... sift you," Jesus said to Peter. The devil knew the disciples were weak at this time. Christ their captain was about to be taken from the head of their regiment. They were discontented among themselves, arguing about who would have the best seat in heaven. And their supply of stronger faith, which the spirit was to bring, had not yet come. Therefore, Christ sent them to Jerusalem to wait together until he could dispatch his spirit to them. This example shows us, in the weakness of our graces, whom to ask for a fresh supply.

He is called "the old serpent," and for good reason: subtle by nature, yet evermore cunning; wrathful by nature, yet evermore enraged. Like a bull the longer he is baited, the madder he grows. And considering what little time he has left, we who are to fight with him must enter the arena well-equipped.

– William Gurnall, *The Christian in Complete Armour*
daily readings in spiritual warfare, Jan. 25

So take everything the Master has set out for you, well-made weapons of the best materials. And put them to use so you will be able to stand up to everything the Devil throws your way. This is no afternoon athletic contest that we'll walk away from and forget about in a couple of hours. This is for keeps, a life-or-death fight to the finish against the Devil and all his angels.
–Ephesians 6:11-12 (The Message)

EXERCISE

Take a businessman to lunch and ask him how you can help or pray for him.

"The desire for safety stands against every noble human endeavor."

– Tacitus

Journal

21

Lord of the Harvest

Sometimes worry is carrying a load that one should not carry at all. I think it was Lyman Beecher who said that he got along very comfortably after he gave up running the universe. Some good earnest people are greatly concerned about the way things in the world are going. I'm obliged to confess to some pretty serious blunders there. It seemed to me that there was so much to be done, so many people needing help, so much of wrong and sin to fight that I must be ever pushing and never sleeping. I had to sleep of course; but all my burden, which meant the burden of the world's need as I saw it, was lugged faithfully to bed every night. There was a lot of pillow-planning. But I found that the wrinkles grew thick, and the physical strength gave out, and yet at the end of vigorous campaigning there seemed about as much left to do as ever.

Then one day my tired eyes lit upon that wondrous phrase, "the lord of the harvest." It caught fire in my heart at once. "Oh! there is a Lord of the harvest," I said to myself. I had been forgetting that. He is a Lord, a masterful one. He has the whole campaign mapped out, and each one's part in helping mapped out too. And I let the responsibility of the campaign lie over where it belonged. When night time came I went to bed to sleep. My pillow was this, "There is a Lord of the harvest."

My keynote came to be obedience to Him. That meant keen ears to hear, keen judgment to understand, keeping quiet so the sound of His voice would always be distinctly heard. It meant trusting Him when things didn't seem to go with a swing. It meant sweet sleep at night, and new strength at the day's beginning. It did not mean any less work. It did seem to mean less fruitless dust.

– SD Gordon, *Quiet Talks on Service*, pp. 164-165

And He said, "The kingdom of God is as if a man should scatter seed on the ground, and should sleep by night and rise by day, and the seed should sprout and grow, he himself does not know how."
– Mark 4:26-27 (NKJV)

EXERCISE

Find an individual or two and spend time intentionally discipling them. Make this a weekly time of open sharing and challenge for growth. Take your eyes off of the crowd and focus on an individual.

"We are not to stop sowing because some of the soil looks unpromising."

– *Eugene Peterson*

Journal

22

The Man Behind the Wall

Then I saw in my dream, that the Interpreter took Christian by the hand, and led him into a place where was a fire burning against a wall. Standing by the wall was an individual continually throwing water on the fire to put it out. Yet the fire just burned higher and hotter.

Christian asked, "What does this mean?"

The Interpreter answered, "This fire is the work of grace working in the heart. He who throws water on it, to extinguish it and put it out, is the devil. But as you see, the fire is burning higher and hotter in spite of it. You'll be shown the reason of it."

With that he took Christian to the other side of the wall. There he saw a man with a vessel of oil in his hand, of the which he did also continually cast (but secretly) into the fire.

Then said Christian, "What means this?"

The Interpreter answered, "This is Christ, who continually, with the oil of his grace, maintains the work already begun in the heart; by the means of which, notwithstanding what the devil can do, the souls of his people prove gracious still. And in that thou sawest that the man stood behind the wall to maintain the fire; this is to teach thee, that it is hard for the tempted to see how this work of grace is maintained in the soul."

– John Bunyan, *Pilgrim's Progress in Modern English*, p. 40

And He said to me, "My grace is sufficient for you, for My strength is made perfect in weakness." Therefore most gladly I will rather boast in my infirmities, that the power of Christ may rest upon me.
– 2 Corinthians 12:9 (NKJV)

EXERCISE

Explain this parable to someone this week.

"The work of the Holy Ghost is often most mighty
when least of its power is seen by the common eye."
                                    –RC Chapman

Journal

23

The Deep Root

If in your case the man is to be at all like his divine message, then you must keep your heart with all diligence; for your outward life before the world will be measured by your inward life with the Lord Jesus Christ. The water in a public fountain never rises one inch higher than its birthplace upon the mountainside.

The greater your piety, the greater your power. Genius, scholarship, eloquence, are no substitutes for whole-souled love of Christ and holiness of life. If you do not love your Master intensely, you will soon get weary of your work; if you do not love your people unselfishly and devotedly, they will soon get weary of you. The deeper you root down into Christ's heart and your people's hearts, the larger and the longer will be your pastorate.

That prince of modern evangelists, Charles G. Finney, used to have seasons when he felt shorn of his spiritual strength. Then he shut himself up with

God, went down on his knees, and, emptying himself of all self-seekings and self-reliance, he fervently prayed to be filled with the Holy Spirit. Then he went to his pulpit like a giant.

– Theodore Cuyler, *The Young Preacher*, pp. 108-109

I have written to you, fathers, Because you have known Him who is from the beginning. I have written to you, young men, Because you are strong, and the word of God abides in you, And you have overcome the wicked one.

– 1 John 2:14 (NKJV)

EXERCISE

Read the biography of a giant of the faith this week.

*"We are never so well prepared for
effectual service to man as when we are
holding fellowship with God."*
— RC Chapman

Journal

24

The Noise of a Fly

"*I throw myself down in my chamber, and I call in, and invite God, and his Angels thither, and when they are there, I neglect God and his Angels, for the noise of a fly, for the rattling of a coach, for the whining of a door.*" (John Donne)

How often have we knelt to pray and before our hearts have even entered into God's presence we become absorbed in some trivial earthly matter. The phone rings, our stomach growls, we remember something we ought to have done. As single-hearted servants we ought to stay focused on the One to whom we are speaking and listening, but we do not always. In the end our faithfulness will not be measured merely by counting up the list of tasks performed. A measure of our faithfulness will be in our attention to the Master Himself, in the keenness of our listening for His Words.

Some are effective and contented contemplatives, not I. It requires rigor and intentionality for me to stay put and listen, and to willingly open my stubborn heart before my Master. Wanting to be aware and sensitive to the needs around me, I often forget that without His detailed instructions, I'll be of little help to those I seek to nurture. How many more years until I learn that the earth can wait a few moments for me to solve all its ills?

As a boy sitting in school I longed for recess times. I would sprint out of the school doors with my friends and run and wrestle and chase until my heart pounded. Now I am the same in some core way. "Sit still", I say to myself, like that lively schoolboy waiting for recess. Maybe I have yet to learn the pure joy of making Him my recess- the place of heart-pounding joy. Come unto me and I will give you recess?

– Richard Earl

You will keep him in perfect peace, Whose mind is stayed on You, Because he trusts in You.
–Isaiah 26:3 (NKJV)

Sometimes, hard-trying, it seems I cannot pray--

For doubt, and pain, and anger, and all strife.

Yet some poor half-fledged prayer-bird from the nest

May fall, flit, fly, perch--crouch in the bowery breast

Of the large, nation-healing tree of life;--

Moveless there sit through all the burning day,

And on my heart at night a fresh leaf cooling lay.

– George MacDonald *Diary of an Old Soul,*
        January 14

EXERCISE

Practice praying without ceasing. Make your life a prayer to God this week. Make every act, every thought, every word an act of faith and a prayer.

Journal

25

Endure Patiently

We must carry on our work with patience. We must bear with many abuses and injuries from those to whom we seek to do good. When we have studied for them, and prayed for them, and exhorted them with all earnestness and condescension, and given them what we are able, and tended them as if they had been our children, we must expect that many of them will repay us with scorn and hatred and contempt, and account us their enemies because we tell them the truth.

Now we must endure all this patiently, and we must unweariedly continue doing good, in meekness instructing those that oppose themselves, "if God perhaps will grant them repentance, so that they may know the truth." We have to deal with distracted men, who will fly in the face of their physician, but we must not, therefore, neglect their cure. He is unworthy to be a physician, who will be driven away from a frenetic patient by foul words.

– Richard Baxter, *The Reformed Pastor*, pp. 180-181

And Hannah prayed and said: "My heart rejoices in the Lord; My horn is exalted in the Lord. I smile at my enemies, Because I rejoice in Your salvation.

– 1 Samuel 2:1 (NKJV)

Keep me from wrath, let it seem ever so right:

My wrath will never work thy righteousness.

Up, up the hill, to the whiter than snow-shine,

Help me to climb, and dwell in pardon's light.

I must be pure as thou, or ever less

Than thy design of me--therefore incline

My heart to take men's wrongs as thou tak'st mine.

– George MacDonald, *Diary of an Old Soul*, February 18

EXERCISE

Write down the names of three persons who have spoken harsh or unkind words to you or your family. Consider the pain they have caused you and then forgive them fully, asking God to bless them and make them allies in the work.

*"Also do not take to heart everything
people say, lest you hear your servant
cursing you."*
— *Ecclesiastes 7:21 (NKJV)*

Journal

26

Knowing Ourselves

The single most important piece of information a leader possesses is self-awareness. The dictionary uses a variety of words to portray the meaning of awareness: knowledge, mindful, vigilance, conscious, alert, to note a few when you add the word self to these, you get a good idea of what self-awareness includes: self-knowledge, self-mindfulness, self-vigilance, self-consciousness, and self-alertness. The discipline of self-awareness then is the leader's intentional quest for self-understanding.

The hazards for leaders of not being self-aware are serious and can even be deadly. Without this insight into themselves and their behavior and motivations, leaders become subject to unknown or underappreciated forces that influence their actions and that can sabotage their work. Without appropriate self-awareness, hidden addictions or compulsions may guide leaders to behaviors that create huge problems and may dismay, exasperate, and bewilder those they lead. Leaders who operate without self-awareness run the risk of being blindsided by destructive impulses and confused by emotions that threaten to derail their agenda and leadership effectiveness. They may overestimate or underestimate their abilities and respond unpredictably. For followers, credibility rises or falls on consistency – something leaders short on self-awareness usually do not have. In short, leaders lacking self-awareness are besieged from within. They often are their own worst enemy. And they don't even know it!

On the other hand leaders who know themselves have gained their best ally – themselves! Self-awareness gifts them with significant insight. They know why they are on the planet and what contribution they intend to make – and they are in hot pursuit of making it. They know the behaviors and values that support their mission they know how to measure their success. They know what they bring to the table in terms of talent and abilities. They know what they don't know, so they are constantly pushing their learning in strategic areas that support their personal growth and missional effectiveness.

– Reggie McNeal, *Practicing Greatness*, pp. 10-11

*Investigate my life, O God, find out everything about
me; Cross-examine and test me, get a clear picture of
what I'm about; See for yourself whether I've done
anything wrong— then guide me on the road to
eternal life.*
    —Psalms 139:23-24 (The Message)

EXERCISE

Take a personality test and ask someone to work
through it with you. (DISC, Taylor/Johnson,
Meyers/Briggs)

Journal

27

Communitas

Many of us crave teamwork, adventure and risk in our leadership environment, but most of the time these are sorely missing. We are caught between our need for stability and success in ministry, and the powerful lure to live an edgier form of Christianity, like we imagine Jesus Himself and the apostles lived.

How many times have we bemoaned the lack of commitment we see from church folks? No matter how hard we promote and cajole, it seems like the same folks always make up the core of volunteers. There must be a better way to carry out Christ's mission. What began as an amazing safari turns into a tedious trip to the zoo.

I think I may have found an answer to this dilemma in what Alan Hirsch and Michael Frost call "Communitas". Dictionary.com defines it as "the sense of sharing and intimacy that develops among persons who experience liminality as a group."

"Liminality" refers to a place of threshold, where a group is out of their normal environment and culture and moving into a new phase of experience.

Communitas describes what I felt in high school on the cold and wet soccer field or in the suffocating wrestling room as my fellow athletes struggled together chasing the elusive goal of greatness. It is found in perhaps its most extreme form on the field of battle, when soldiers very lives depend upon their intimate relationships with their comrades. Have you ever wondered why we have not found a greater sense of teamwork and closeness in church life, even among peers in our denominations? Many have found most relationships to be pretty much surface level, and cooperation to be short-lived.

As a fraternity brother in the 1970's the pursuit of communitas in the house was very intentional. In fact, it was the main goal when bringing new members into the house. The hazing and rituals were all about creating a "brotherhood" through liminality. While Christ's methods and goals are very different from those of a secular fraternity, lessons can be drawn from what they are able to achieve.

There have been times when I felt a greater sense of communitas, as opposed to the shallow and paltry sense of "community" we usually end up with in the church context. Short-term missions trips produce this level of relationship because they place us in a foreign environment with limited resources and uncertain outcomes. Folks feel united, exhilarated and renewed after such an experience, and are generally disappointed when they return to "normal" church.

But I have identified a few other practical ways to promote and create communitas in our churches and lives. Group fasting creates a type of communitas, as do retreats, certain types of small groups, spiritual discipline groups, and intentional missional outreaches. Articulating purpose and vision and plunging into it with others is what these ordeals are all about, and they energize people. There are innumerable ways to do this.

The idea of liminality is crucial because while we go to great lengths to make people comfortable in church, the way to intimacy and greater commitment may lie in calling them, counter intuitively, to a higher level of separation and sacrifice- making them uncomfortable. Paul had communitas in the churches he planted, and in his planting team. Jesus had it with His disciples, and when given the chance to opt out of it they replied, "Master, to whom would we go? You have the words of real life, eternal life." John 6:68

– Richard Earl

*After these things the Lord appointed seventy others
also, and sent them two by two before His face into
every city and place where He Himself was about to go.
Then He said to them, "The harvest truly is great, but*

the laborers are few; therefore pray the Lord of the harvest to send out laborers into His harvest. Go your way; behold, I send you out as lambs among wolves. Carry neither money bag, knapsack, nor sandals; and greet no one along the road. But whatever house you enter, first say, 'Peace to this house.' And if a son of peace is there, your peace will rest on it; if not, it will return to you. And remain in the same house, eating and drinking such things as they give, for the laborer is worthy of his wages. Do not go from house to house. Whatever city you enter, and they receive you, eat such things as are set before you. And heal the sick there, and say to them, 'The kingdom of God has come near to you.'"

–Luke 10:1-9 (NKJV)

EXERCISE

Present a project to your leadership that will help increase Communitas in your church.

"Everybody here wants a revolution, but nobody here wants to do the dishes."

                  – Shane Claiborne

Journal

28

Small Service

God sets some men on the high places of the earth and appoints them to exciting challenges. But he orders others to pitch their tents on lower ground and not be ashamed of their assignment, no matter how inferior it seems. Now to encourage us to be faithful in our particular place, God has big promises which apply to them all. And his promises are like the beams of the Sun: they shine as freely through the window of the poor man's cottage as through the prince's Palace.

God's promises strengthen our hands and hearts against the discouragement that is most likely to weaken us in his service. They support and guard us against the furious opposition of an angry world: "I will not fail thee, nor forsake thee. Be strong and of good courage." (Joshua 1:5-6) This was a promise God gave to Israel's chief magistrate. And the ministers promise agrees with it, having generally the same trials, enemies, and discouragements: "go ye therefore, and teach all nations;... and well, I am with you always, even unto the end of the world." (Matt 28:19-20)

To arm us against discontent and discouragement, God promises as great a reward in the most menial service as He gives in more honorable service. Is anything more degrading than the role of a slave? Yet nothing less than heaven itself is promised to the faithful servant.

– William Gurnall from *The Christian in Complete Armour* daily readings in spiritual warfare
  November 16

Whatever you do, work heartily, as for the Lord and not for men, knowing that from the Lord you will receive the inheritance as your reward. You are serving the Lord Christ.
> – *Colossians 3:23-24 (ESV)*

EXERCISE

Invite someone to church without disclosing that you pastor a church.

*"Gather my insufficiencies and place
them in Your hands."*

– *Relient K*

Journal

29

Losing the Mystery

The ministry is one of the most perilous of professions. The devil hates the Spirit-filled minister with an intensity second only to that which he feels for Christ Himself. The source of this hatred is not difficult to discover. An effective, Christlike minister is a constant embarrassment to the devil, a threat to his dominion, a rebuttal of his best arguments and a dogged reminder of his coming overthrow. No wonder he hates him.

Satan knows that the downfall of a prophet of God is a strategic victory for him, so he rests not day or night devising hidden snares and deadfalls for the ministry. Perhaps a better figure would be the poison dart that only paralyzes its victim, for I think that Satan has little interest in killing the preacher outright. An ineffective, half-alive minister is a better advertisement for hell than a good man dead. So the preacher's dangers are likely to be spiritual rather than physical, though sometimes the enemy works through bodily weaknesses to get to the preacher's soul.

There are indeed some very real dangers of the grosser sort which the minister must guard against, such as love of money and women; but the deadliest perils are far more subtle than these. So let's concentrate on them.

There is, for one, the danger that the minister shall come to think of himself as belonging to a privileged class...Seeing whose name he bears, the unconscious acceptance of belonging to a privileged class is particularly incongruous for the minister. Christ came to give, to serve, to sacrifice and to die, and said to His disciples, "As my Father hath sent me, even so send I you." The preacher is a servant of the Lord and of the people. He is in great moral peril when he forgets this.

Another danger is that he may develop a per-functory spirit in the performance of the work of the Lord. Familiarity may breed contempt even at the very altar of God. How frightful a thing it is for the preacher when he becomes accustomed to his work, when his sense of wonder departs, when he gets used to the unusual, when he loses his solemn fear in the presence of the High and Holy One; when, to put it bluntly, he gets a little bored with God and heavenly things.

If anyone should doubt that this can happen let him read the Old Testament and see how the priests of Jehovah sometimes lost their sense of divine mystery and became profane even as they performed their holy duties. And church history reveals that this tendency toward perfunctoriness did not die with the passing of the Old Testament order. Secular priests and pastors who keep the doors of God's house for bread are still among us. Satan will see to it that they are, for they do the cause of God more injury than a whole army of atheists would do.

– AW Tozer, *God Tells the man who cares*, pp. 76-77

Then Nadab and Abihu, the sons of Aaron, each took his censer and put fire in it, put incense on it, and offered profane fire before the Lord, which He had not commanded them. So fire went out from the Lord and devoured them, and they died before the Lord.
And Moses said to Aaron, "This is what the Lord spoke, saying: 'By those who come near Me I must be regarded as holy; And before all the people I must be glorified.'"
So Aaron held his peace.
– Leviticus 10:1-3(KJV)

EXERCISE

In an effort to avoid over familiarity with the things of God and church try corresponding, counseling or studying in a public place like a coffee shop, park or library.

Journal

30

What the World Wants

When the Good Shepherd appeared in Galilee, the contrast between him and the other shepherds was perceived at once. There was sympathy in Jesus' tone and gentleness in his touch which proved at once that he was with the people in their sorrows and upward strivings. The chief trouble with the modern church is that in too many localities it has lost contact with the life of the town. It is out of touch with the souls of men in their present perplexities and needs, and hence it cannot influence them.

The impression is abroad that Christianity is a pretty speech, a bit of idealism, a lovely dream, a stanza of poetry, a piece of Sunday acting, something that the preacher can say by rote, and to which the saints can say, "Amen"; and not a sober, serious, week-day life. What the world most wants today is shepherding. The world has many comforts, luxuries in abundance; what it lacks is love. Love cannot be satisfactorily expressed to our generation in printer's ink, in evangelistic appeals, in pulpit eloquence, or in doctrinal statements. The expression which the world now demands is the love of the shepherd who takes the lambs in his bosom, who gently leads those who have their young, and who day by day lays down his life for the sheep. A generation ago the word of God was the Bible, today the word of God is Jesus and the man who has the spirit of Jesus. A genuine Christian is the only epistle which the world now cares to read. Multitudes care little for worship, less for church polity, still less for creeds, nothing for traditions and ceremonies. Character is everything. Shepherding work is the work for which humanity is crying.

– Charles Jefferson, *The Minister as Shepherd*, pp. 103-104

" *I'll set shepherd-leaders over them who will take good care of them. They won't live in fear or panic anymore. All the lost sheep rounded up!*" *God's Decree.*
– *Jeremiah 23:4 (The Message)*

EXERCISE

Visit a shut-in or "wandering sheep" whom you have not seen in a while. Endeavor to simply shepherd them as opposed to getting them to return to church.

"*The differences between the orator &*
prophet are many & radical, the chief
being that an orator speaks for himself,
while a prophet speaks for God."
                                    –AW Tozer

Journal

31

Go to Them

Do you want to know how you can reach the masses? Go to their homes and enter into sympathy with them; tell them you have come to do them good, and let them see that you have a heart to feel for them. When they find out that you really love them, all those things that are in their hearts against God and against Christianity will be swept out of the way. Atheists may tell them that you only want to get their money, and that you do not really care for their happiness. We have to contradict that lie by our lives, and send it back to the pit where it came from,

We are not going to do it unless we go personally to them and prove that we really love them. There are hundreds and thousands of families that could easily be reached if we had thousands of Christians going to them and entering into sympathy with their sorrows. That is what they want. This poor world is groaning and sighing for sympathy—human sympathy. I am quite sure it was that in Christ's life which touched the hearts of the common people. He made Himself one with them. He who was rich for our sakes became poor. He was born in the manger so that He might put himself on a level with the lowest of the low.

I think that in this matter He teaches His disciples a lesson. He wants us to convince the world that He is their friend. They do not believe it. If once the world were to grasp this thought, that Jesus Christ is the Friend of the sinner, they would soon flock to Him. I am sure that ninety-nine in every hundred of those out of Christ think that, instead of loving them, God hates them. How are they to find out their mistake? They do not attend our churches; and if they did there are many places where they would not hear it. Do you think that if those poor harlots walking the streets of our cities really believed that Jesus Christ loved them and wanted to be their friend—that if He were here in person He would not condemn them, but would take sides with them, and try to lift them up—they would go on in their sins ? Do you think the poor drunkard who reels along the street really believes that Christ is his friend and loves him? … This story of the good Samaritan is given to teach us this lesson. Let us publish abroad the good news that Christ loves sinners, and came into the world that He might save them.

– DL Moody, *To the Work*, pp. 28-29

Then Levi gave Him a great feast in his own house.
And there were a great number of tax collectors and
others who sat down with them. And their scribes and
the Pharisees complained against His disciples, saying,
"Why do You eat and drink with tax collectors and
sinners?" Jesus answered and said to them, "Those who
are well have no need of a physician, but those who are
sick. I have not come to call the righteous, but sinners,
to repentance."

–*Luke 5:29-32 (NKJV)*

EXERCISE

Spend some time this week with people far away from God. Listen to them.

Journal

The Golden Pipe

We are constantly on a stretch, if not on the strain, to devise new methods, new plans, new organizations to advance the church and secure enlargement and efficiency for the gospel. This trend of the day has a tendency to lose sight of the man or sink the man in the plan or organization. God's plan is to make much of the man, far more of him than of anything else. Men are God's message. The church is looking for better methods; God is looking for better men.

"There was a man sent from God whose name was John." The dispensation that heralded and prepared the way for Christ was bound up in that man John. "Unto us a child is born, unto us a son is given." The world's salvation comes out of that cradled son. When Paul appeals to the personal character of the men who routed the gospel in the world, he solves the mystery of their success. The glory and efficiency of the gospel is staked on the people who proclaim it. When God declares that the eyes of the Lord went to and fro throughout the whole Earth to show Him so strong on behalf of them whose heart is perfect toward him, he declares the necessity of man and his dependence on them as a channel through which to exert its power upon the world.

What the Church needs to-day is not more machinery or better, not new organizations or more and novel methods, but men whom the Holy Ghost can use—men of prayer, men mighty in prayer. The Holy Ghost does not flow through methods, but through men. He does not come on machinery, but on men. He does not anoint plans, but men—men of prayer...

The character as well as the fortunes of the gospel is committed to the preacher. He makes or mars the message from God to man. The preacher is the golden pipe through which the divine oil flows. The pipe must not only be golden, but open and flawless, that the oil may have a full, unhindered, unwasted flow.

The man makes the preacher. God must make the man. The messenger is, if possible, more than the message. The preacher is more than the sermon. The preacher makes the sermon. As the life-giving milk from the mother's bosom is but the mother's life, so all the preacher says is tinctured, impregnated by what the preacher is. The treasure is in earthen vessels, and the taste of the vessel impregnates and may discolor. The man, the whole man, lies behind the sermon. Preaching is not the performance of an hour. It is the outflow of a life. It takes twenty years to make a sermon, because it takes twenty years to make the man. The true sermon is a thing of life. The sermon grows because the man grows. The sermon is forceful because the man is forceful. The sermon is holy because the man is holy. The sermon is full of the divine unction because the man is full of the divine unction.

– EM Bounds, *The Preacher and Prayer*, pp. 5-13

You've all been to the stadium and seen the athletes race. Everyone runs; one wins. Run to win. All good athletes train hard. They do it for a gold medal that tarnishes and fades. You're after one that's gold eternally. I don't know about you, but I'm running hard for the finish line. I'm giving it everything I've got. No sloppy living for me! I'm staying alert and in top condition. I'm not going to get caught napping, telling everyone else all about it and then missing out myself.
– *1 Corinthians 9:24-27 (The Message)*

EXERCISE

Ask a close friend to share with you your three greatest strengths and weaknesses. Be ready to hear them clearly and respond instead of react.

Journal

33

Utterance

And for me, that utterance may be given to me, that I
may open my mouth boldly to make known the mystery
of the gospel
                                    – Ephesians 6:19 (NKJV)

In this verse Paul was asking prayer that utterance may be given. On his own admission he was no orator. In his mental scrap with the intellectuals on Mars Hill, he heard the wise men ask, "what will this babbler say?" (Acts 17:18). His letters they say, are weighty and strong; but his bodily presence is weak, and his speech of no account (2 Corinthians 10:10). Paul could have omitted this slight to himself, but he cheerfully states both their contempt for his scarred body and also their low rating of his speech.

Jesus had utterance. When officers returning from Jesus to the Pharisees said of the master, "never man spake like this man," they were not referring to eloquence or wisdom. Again in Gethsemane, officers from the chief priests were unable to arrest the defenseless son of God because he had authority. He simply said, "I am he," and men fell as if smitten by lightning. I believe a transition of power from his very lips slew these men. Even his critics said, "He speaks as one having authority and not like the scribes" (Matthew 7:29).

Jock Purves, a beloved Scotchman once told me he thought the greatest thing that John Knox ever did was to dismiss his congregation one morning in St. Kyles Cathedral because he had no message for them. Most of us would have warmed up an old sermon or stammered through a few scattered thoughts. But Knox wanted the utterance.

Finally, the story is told of the young minister who once had to substitute for a more famous colleague — always an unenviable task. When the people were asked what they thought of the unnamed herald, one of them replied cryptically, "I've often heard a better preacher, but I've never heard a preacher better." Evidently, that messenger had utterance.

– Leonard Ravenhill, *Meat for Men*, pp. 85-88

EXERCISE

Determine to never offer counsel without an accompanying excerpt from the Word of God. Gain force in your exhorting by allowing the Word of God to sharpen the blade of your plowing.

"A man may study because his brain is hungry for knowledge. But he prays because his soul is hungry for God"

–L. Ravenhill

Journal

34

The Angry Grocer

To forgive without upbraiding, even by manner or look, is a high exercise of grace— it is imitation of Christ. -RC Chapman

To be sure, not everyone liked Robert Chapman. One such person, a grocer in Barnstaple, became so upset at Chapman's open-air preaching that he spit on him! For a number of years, the grocer continued to attack and castigate Chapman. Yet Chapman continued on in his ministry and, when the opportunity presented itself, reached out to bless the grocer.

The opportunity arose when one of Chapman's wealthy relatives visited him in Barnstaple. The visit was more than just a social call; the relative wanted to try to understand what Chapman was doing. When he arrived at the house by horse-drawn cab, he couldn't believe that the well-bred Chapman lived in such a modest home in an impoverished neighborhood. Yet Chapman warmly invited him into his clean, simple home. As they talked, Chapman explained what it meant to live in dependence on the Lord and shared how the Lord always met his needs. As the relative was leaving, he asked if he could buy groceries for Chapman, who gladly agreed. But Chapman insisted that the groceries be purchased at a certain grocer's shop—yes, the grocer who had so vehemently maligned him.

Ignorant of previous interactions between the grocer and Chapman, the relative went where he was directed. He selected and paid for a large amount of food, and then told the grocer to deliver it to R. C. Chapman. The stunned grocer told the visitor that he must have come to the wrong shop, but the visitor explained that Chapman had sent him specifically to that shop. Soon the grocer arrived at Chapman's house, where he broke down in tears and asked for forgiveness. That very day the grocer yielded his life to Christ!

We can hardly begin to imagine what God will do when His people truly love as Christ loved!

– Robert L. Peterson and Alexander Strauch, *Agape Leadership*, pp. 39-40

You're familiar with the old written law, "Love your friend," and its unwritten companion, "Hate your enemy." I'm challenging that. I'm telling you to love your enemies. Let them bring out the best in you, not the worst. When someone gives you a hard time,

respond with the energies of prayer, for then you are
working out of your true selves, your God-created
selves. This is what God does. He gives his best—the
sun to warm and the rain to nourish—to everyone,
regardless: the good and bad, the nice and nasty. If all
you do is love the lovable, do you expect a bonus?
Anybody can do that. If you simply say hello to those
who greet you, do you expect a medal? Any run-of-the-
mill sinner does that. In a word, what I'm saying is,
Grow up. You're kingdom subjects. Now live like it.
Live out your God-created identity. Live generously
and graciously toward others, the way God lives
toward you.
— Matthew 5:43-48 (The Message)

EXERCISE

Make it your practice to allow your soft answer
to turn away the harsh words or actions of others.
Find someone who does not deserve your kindness
and bless them today.

Journal

35

The Rambunctious One

Author Margaret Feinberg spent some time with a shepherdess and her flock in Washington State to learn some deeper lessons of the relationship between shepherd and sheep so often referenced in scripture. Here is some of what she learned. The parallels for those in ministry should be self-evident.

As the various sheep grew braver with me, I became more courageous with them. While I made sure one hand was full of grain, I used the other to caress their foreheads and feel their fleeces. I found the contact with the sheep not only soothing to the animals, but also to me.

I noticed a tiny ewe lamb the color of fresh snow. I wanted to cuddle the lovable baby lamb, but its protective mother intentionally kept it away from the other sheep—and us.

"Is that Opal?" I asked.

"Yes!" Lynne said, pleased that I was already able to identify one of her sheep. "She's the protective one guarding Swan." "May I pet Swan?" I asked.

Lynne leaned against the gate for a moment, looking at Opal with steady eyes. "Not until the mother is ready. Opal doesn't even want me around Swan yet."

As the treat supply dwindled, so did the surrounding sheep. Many returned to the edges of the field to graze, but a few remained, each taking a turn to be scratched beneath the chin before moving aside to let another sheep in.

Angry that he wasn't the center of attention, one of the young rams, Alano, began butting me with his horns. The first time was reasonably gentle, but I still gave Alano the stink eye. He stepped back. We locked eyes; he took a few more steps backward, then made a running start toward me. The winsomeness of the moment vanished.

"Lynne!" I cried out.

"You can't let him do that," she said sternly. "Grab him by the horn."

I reached out, clenched my fist around one of his curved horns, and held Alano at arm's length. "No!" I said firmly, as if I was disciplining my dog, Hershey. Foolishly thinking the ram had lost his machismo at the sound of my firm rebuke, I released Alano. He took a few steps back and rammed me again.

"He has to be disciplined now," Lynne said, grabbing the rambunctious ram by the horn.

Dragging Alano into another fenced section, she placed him in isolation from the other sheep,

Lynne returned to the grass beside me, and together we watched as Alano stood pitifully at the gate, his baa-aa's sounding more like moans. Alano was one unhappy ram. But if he didn't learn, Lynne's next course of action would be neutering him; a surgery that would transform Alano into what Lynne called "a tame lawn mower."

"If I don't discipline him now, he will grow up to be dangerous and of no use to anyone" Lynne explained. "He's sitting by the gate because he hates being alone. That's why he's crying."

"So that's what a sheep in time-out looks like!"

I had read that some shepherds use time-outs and others use squirt bottles to try to discipline their sheep. If a ram grows up with no fear of its shepherd and no respect for other sheep, the most humane act is to slaughter it. Lynne confirmed this. An unruly ram will hurt or kill others if it isn't destroyed.

"My rams need to respect me and know who I am," Lynne explained. "It's normal for rams to want to bash objects, which is why I give them balls and other toys. But make no mistake, an uncontrollable ram can cause immense damage to a flock. They need to know I am to be respected."

– Margaret Feinberg, *Scouting the Divine*, pp. 31-32

This charge I commit to you, son Timothy, according to the prophecies previously made concerning you, that by them you may wage the good warfare, having faith and a good conscience, which some having rejected, concerning the faith have suffered shipwreck, of whom are Hymenaeus and Alexander, whom I delivered to Satan that they may learn not to blaspheme.

– 1 Timothy 1:18-20 (KJV)

EXERCISE

Explore passages from scripture that deal with church discipline. How can you be more intentional about bringing restoration through correction?

"Don't count your critics, weigh them."
— *Reggie McNeal*

Journal

A Little Company

Anyone who has been involved with church planting or revitalization on any level knows what a gargantuan task it is to plant and grow a young church or to renew an old one. The handbooks for how to do it are as the sands of the sea, but the multiplicity of contexts for this missionary work makes them only marginally useful.

Likewise with church transformation. The task of taking a church from stagnation to genuine life is herculean at the least. A bit of simple and sound advice and encouragement according to Biblical patterns is welcome indeed.

I found such help in the timeworn and humble pages of Matthew Henry's Concise Commentary and it has helped clarify my vision. Here is what good Brother Henry said in his commentary on Acts Chapters 1:12-14: "A little company united in love, exemplary in their conduct, fervent in prayer, and wisely zealous to promote the cause of Christ, are likely to increase rapidly."

It is a pattern to follow, forged out of decades of fruitful ministry experience. There are exceptions to this rule, it is not hard and fast. Love, holiness, prayerful, zealous and united we must be or we fail to imitate our Master Jesus, and have no right to expect He will want to see our model duplicated or our influence expanded.

– Richard Earl with thanks to Matthew Henry

Then they returned to Jerusalem from the mount called Olivet, which is near Jerusalem, a Sabbath day's journey. And when they had entered, they went up into the upper room where they were staying: Peter, James, John, and Andrew; Philip and Thomas; Bartholomew and Matthew; James the son of Alphaeus and Simon the Zealot; and Judas the son of James. These all continued with one accord in prayer and supplication, with the women and Mary the mother of Jesus, and with His brothers.

–Acts 1:12-14 (NKJV)

EXERCISE

Contact the pastor of a church plant or struggling church and take him to lunch. Find ways to bless and encourage him/her.

"Many pray for seats to be filled by incoming sinners, while I often pray for them to be emptied by the outgoing saints."

        –Anthony Brabazon

Journal

37

The Heavenly Vision

From that time many of His disciples went back, and walked no more with Him.

– John 6:66

When God gives a vision by His Spirit through His word of what He wants, and your mind and soul thrill to it, if you do not walk in the light of that vision, you will sink into servitude to a point of view which Our Lord never had. Disobedience in mind to the heavenly vision will make you a slave to points of view that are alien to Jesus Christ. Do not look at someone else and say— "Well, if he can have those views and prosper, why cannot I?" You have to walk in the light of the vision that has been given to you and not compare yourself with others or judge them, that is between them and God. When you find that a point of view in which you have been delighting clashes with the heavenly vision and you debate, certain things will begin to develop in you—a sense of property and a sense of personal right, things of which Jesus Christ made nothing. He was always against these things as being the root of everything alien to Himself. "A man's life consists not in the abundance of the things that he possesses." If we do not recognize this, it is because we are ignoring the undercurrent of Our Lord's teaching.

We are apt to lie back and bask in the memory of the wonderful experience we have had. If there is one standard in the New Testament revealed by the light of God and you do not come up to it, and do not feel inclined to come up to it, that is the beginning of backsliding, because it means your conscience does not answer to the truth. You can never be the same after the unveiling of a truth. That moment marks you for going on as a more true disciple of Jesus Christ, or for going back as a deserter.

– Oswald Chambers, *Called of God*

Therefore, King Agrippa, I was not disobedient to the heavenly vision.

–Acts 26:19 (NKJV)

EXERCISE

Ask three people this week to define what they believe to be your vision for ministry.

*"Victory begins with the name of Jesus
on our lips. It is consummated with the
nature of Jesus in our hearts."*
         —Francis Frangipane

Journal

38

Spirit of the Prophet

I will wait upon the Lord, that hideth His face from
the house of Jacob; and I will look for Him.
– Isaiah 8:17

Here we have a servant of God, waiting upon Him, not on behalf of himself, but of his people, from whom God was hiding His face. It suggests to us how our waiting upon God, though it commences with our personal needs, with the desire for the revelation of Himself, or of the answer to personal petitions, need not, may not, stop there. We may be walking in the full light of God's countenance, and God yet be hiding His face from His people around us; far from our being content to think that this is nothing but the just punishment of their sin, or the consequence of their indifference, we are called with tender hearts to think of their sad estate, and to wait on God on their behalf.

The privilege of waiting upon God is one that brings great responsibility. Even as Christ, when He entered God's presence, at once used His place of privilege and honor as intercessor, so we, no less, if we know what it is really to enter in and wait upon God, must use our access for our less favored brethren. "I will wait upon the Lord, who hideth His face from the house of Jacob,"

...Do believe that God can help and will help. Let the spirit of the prophet come into you, as you value His words, and set yourself to wait on God, on behalf of His erring children. Instead of the tone of judgment or condemnation, of despondency or despair, realize your calling to wait upon God. If others fail in doing it, give yourself doubly to it. The deeper the darkness, the greater the need of appealing to the one and only Deliverer. The greater the self-confidence around you, that knows not that it is poor and wretched and blind, the more urgent the call on you who profess to see the evil and to have access to Him who alone can help, to be at your post waiting upon God. Say on each new occasion, when you are tempted to speak or to sigh: "I will wait on the Lord, Who hideth His face from the house of Jacob."

– Andrew Murray, *Waiting on God*, pp. 84-86

EXERCISE

The next time you receive a call from someone in need of food or clothing buy the items yourself and deliver them without inviting the family to church. Simply love them and ask what else you could do to help.

Journal

39

Posing Shepherds

I recall vividly the love, loyalty, and undivided devotion of the Masai in East Africa to their animals. For the years we lived among them I never ceased to marvel at the incredible fortitude of these people in providing the best care they could for their livestock. No price was too high to pay to protect that stock from predators. Why? Because they owned them they had a stake in them. They loved them. They were not hirelings.

Just a few days after we moved into the Masai tribe, a small, slim boy about ten years old was carried up to our house. He had, single-handed, tackled a young lioness that tried to kill one of his flock. In total self-abandonment and utter bravery he had managed to spear the lion. The mauling he took almost cost him his life. We rushed him to the nearest hospital twenty-seven miles away where his young life was spared, as by a thread. But why did he do this? Because the sheep were his. His love and honor and loyalty were at stake. He would not spare himself. He was not a hireling.

God has, all through history, entrusted the care of His sheep to so-called undershepherds. And not all of them have proven to be as loyal as the Masai lad, nor as brave as young David, later Israel's great king, who slew the lion and the bear that came to raid his father's flock.

Inevitably in the nature of human affairs there appear those who pretend to be genuine but are not. The ancient prophets of Israel cried out again and again against those who posed as shepherds to God's people, but who instead only plundered them for their own selfish ends.

"And the word of the Lord came unto me, saying, son of man, prophesy against the shepherds of Israel, prophesy, and say unto them, Thus saith the Lord God unto the shepherds; Woe be to the shepherds of Israel that do feed themselves! Should not the Shepherds feed the flocks?" (Ezekiel 34:1-6)

– Philip Keller, *A Shepherd looks at the Good Shepherd and His sheep*, pp. 114-116

EXERCISE

Do as many things as possible for one day this week that do not involve planning, strategy, meetings or money. Focus on people only. Fast the macro stuff so you can do the micro stuff.

"Be not angry that you cannot make
others as you wish them to be since you
cannot make yourself as you wish to be."
　　　　　　　　　　– Thomas a Kempis

Journal

40

Leadership's Price

To aspire to leadership in God's kingdom requires us to be willing to pay a price higher than others are willing to pay. The toll of true leadership is heavy, and the more effective the leader-ship, the greater the cost.

Quinton Hogg, founder of the London Polytechnic Institute, devoted a fortune to the enterprise. Asked how much it had cost to build the great institution, Hogg replied, "Not very much, simply one man's life blood."

That is the price of every great achievement, and it is not paid in a lump sum. Achievement is bought on the time-payment plan, with a new installment required each day. The drain on resources is con-tinuous, and when payments cease, leadership wanes. Our Lord taught that we could not save ourselves in the task of offering salvation to others. When Jesus said, "For whoever wants to save his life will lose it, but whoever loses his life for me will find it." (Matthew 16:25), part of what He meant has to do with hoarding personal resources in the vain hope that they will preserve us.

Samuel Brengle wrote: Spiritual power is the outpouring of spiritual life, and like all life, from that of the moss and lichen on the wall to that of the archangel before the throne, it is from God. Therefore those who aspire to leadership may pay the price, and seek it from God.

This part of the cost must be paid daily. A cross stands in the path of spiritual leadership, and the leader must take it up. "Jesus Christ laid down his life for us. And we ought to lay down our lives for our brothers" (1 John 3:16). To the degree the cross of Christ is across our shoulders and over our backs, so the resurrection life of Christ is manifest through us. No cross, no leadership. Paul declared, "I die every day" (1 Corinthians 15:31b).

Each of the heroes of faith Hebrews 11 was called to sacrifice as part of his or her service. They who lead the church are marked by a willingness to give up personal preferences, to surrender legitimate and natural desires for the sake of God.

Bruce Barton quotes a sign at a service station: "We will crawl under your car oftener and get ourselves dirtier than any of our competition." That is the kind of service the Christian seeks to give.

– Oswald Sanders, *Spiritual Leadership*, pp. 115-116

These all died in faith, not having received the promises, but having seen them afar off were assured of them, embraced them and confessed that they were strangers and pilgrims on the earth.

— Hebrews 11:13 (KJV)

EXERCISE

Choose to fill a void of leadership in your community. Find a great need and organize a small group to meet the need.

Journal

41

Passion or Profession

Whenever the work of the ministry is considered a profession and not a passion, failure is inevitable. To be professional is to be formal; to preach with a passion is to turn men towards God.

I once heard Dr. Grenfell say that the difference between doctors might be indicated as follows: one doctor carries on his work professionally; the other doctor does his work with a passion; and then speaking of his own great ministry to the deep-sea fishermen on the coast of Labrador, he told how he would journey across the ice, with the weather bitterly cold and the traveling dangerous, to set a boy's broken leg or to minister to a patient tossing with a fever; and one could easily see how in his work he felt that he was just as truly preaching Christ as if he stood behind the pulpit in a church.

There must be a consuming passion on the part of the minister if his work is to be pleasing to God.

Sometimes ministers fail because they have a wrong idea of approach to people. There are two ways of approach to the life of the one whom we would influence. The first is by the way of the head. In such an approach there must be argument, and people are rarely argued into the Kingdom of God, for the things of God in the final analysis are spiritually discerned and not intellectually: that is, men may think their way up to the boundary line of the Kingdom, but they pass into the Kingdom by faith.

The second way of approach is by means of the heart. The greatest preachers have been the men who have used the simplest forms of speech. Moody preached so that everybody could understand him. It is said that one day he was pleading with men to come to Christ. Stretching forth his arms toward his congregation he kept saying, "Come! Come!!" and he said it so persuasively and so naturally that a little child climbed down from his mother's lap and started towards Mr. Moody, thinking that the great preacher was calling him. Such preaching is always powerful.

– J. Wilbur Chapman, *The Minister's Handicap*, pp. 64-66

But we were gentle among you, just as a nursing mother cherishes her own children. So, affectionately longing for you, we were well pleased to impart to you not only the gospel of God, but also our own lives,

because you had become dear to us. For you remember,
brethren, our labor and toil; for laboring night and
day, that we might not be a burden to any of you, we
preached to you the gospel of God. You are witnesses,
and God also, how devoutly and justly and blamelessly
we behaved ourselves among you who believe; as you
know how we exhorted, and comforted, and charged
every one of you, as a father does his own children,
that you would walk worthy of God who calls you into
His own kingdom and glory.
　　　　　　　　– 1 Thessalonians 2:7-12 (NKJV)

EXERCISE

Work on discovering great stories for use in your
sermons. Make an effort to appeal to the heart of
your hearers as well as their minds.

Journal

42

He Saw Them Toiling

George MacDonald describes the scene when Jesus went up on the mountain to pray while His disciples rowed across the Sea of Galilee. Jesus saw them toiling, working hard but getting nowhere, and came to bring help...

Now this mountain on which he was praying had a small lake at the foot of it – that is, about 13 miles long, and 5 miles broad. Not wanting his usual companions to be with him this evening – partly, I presume, because they were of the same mind as those who desired to make Him king – yet sent them away in the boat, to go across this water to the other side, where were their homes and their families.

Now, it was not pitch dark either on a mountaintop or on the water down below; yet I doubt if any other man than he would have been keen-eyed enough to discover that little boat down in the middle of the lake, much distressed by the West wind that blew right in their teeth. But He loved every man in it so much, that I think even as He was talking to His Father His eyes would now and then go looking for and finding it – watching it on its way across to the other side.

You must remember it was a little boat; and there are often tremendous storms upon these little lakes with great mountains about them. For the wind will come all at once, rushing down through the clefts in as sudden as squall as ever overtook a sailor at sea...He saw them worn out at the oar, toiling in rowing, for the wind was contrary to them.

So the time for loneliness and prayer was over, and the time to go down out of his secret chamber and help his brethren was come. He did not need to turn and say goodbye to His Father, as if He dwelt on that mountaintop alone: His Father was down there on the lake as well. He went straight down. Could not His Father, if He too was down on the lake, help them without him? Yes. But He wanted Him to do it, that they might see that He did it. Otherwise they could only have thought that the wind fell and the waves lay down, without supposing for a moment that the Master or His Father had had anything to do with it. They would have done just as people do nowadays: they think that the help comes of itself instead of by the will of Him who determined from the first that men should be helped...

At length, when there were nearly worn out, taking feebler and feebler strokes, sometimes missing the water altogether, at other times burying their oars in it up to the handles – as they rose on the crest of the wave, one of them gave a cry, and they all stopped rowing and stared, leaning forward to peer through the darkness. And through the spray which the wind tore from the tops of the waves and scattered before it like dust, they saw, perhaps 100 yards or so from the boat, something standing up from the surface of the water. It seemed to move towards them. It was a shaped like a man. They all cried out with fear, as was natural for the thought that it must be a ghost...

But then, over the noise of the wind and the waters, came the voice they knew so well. It said, "Be of good cheer, it is I. Be not afraid."

– George MacDonald, "He saw them toiling" from *God's Word to His Children*, pp. 14-17

Walk with me and work with me—watch how I do it.
Learn the unforced rhythms of grace. I won't lay
anything heavy or ill-fitting on you. Keep company
with me and you'll learn to live freely and lightly.
– Matthew 11:29-30 (The Message)

EXERCISE

Look for an unsung hero in your church and one in your community-one who has been busy toiling at the oars. Send them a note of appreciation or take them to lunch to show your gratitude for their faithful work.

Journal

43

Oxygen Masks

Every time I fly on a commercial plane I have to listen to this dumb statement: "Before helping someone else with their oxygen mask, put yours on first." I usually tune this announcement out. But one day, I didn't. Instead, I found myself running through my head the reasons why airline personnel are so paranoid about us putting on our own oxygen mask first.

Surely if the person sitting beside me couldn't get his or her mask on and appeared in trouble, I should put his or hers on first. But the more I thought about it the more I realized they had a point. To not put mine on first could be a fatal mistake. You see, if the person next to me needed my help putting the mask on, something else was wrong with him or her. He or she was too weak or confused or hurt to put it on and, even if I got his or hers on, more than likely the person would not be able to help me put mine on and I would probably pass out before putting on my own mask.

Whereas, if I quickly put mine on, the odds are I would be able to get his or hers on in time since I was strong enough to help myself in the first place. Now, what do oxygen masks have to do with rediscovering ministry? Everything!...

Remember—you can't give what you don't have. If you hope to develop spiritual giants, you must be a spiritual giant. If your dream is to develop a group of committed disciples who will turn the world upside down, your commitment must be off the charts. If you want courageous Christians who will venture out on faith and risk it all, you must have the kind of courage that inspires others to be willing to risk it all. You can't give what you don't have.

A lack of spiritual oxygen is the primary reason so many of our churches function more like hospices and funeral homes than the church we see in the New Testament. This deprivation of spiritual oxygen is why more and more Christians are falling victim to various forms of addiction. This lack of spiritual oxygen explains why so many pastors are reaching the end of their ministry burned out and bitter and why so many Christians have little more to show for their faith than a backside that is contoured to the church pews and a brain fried from too many meetings.

No organization, not even a church, ever has more vitality than those who lead it. If the leaders are starving for spiritual oxygen, then so are those they lead. The problem today with most segments of established Christianity is that our leaders are stunted spiritually. It's time for Christians to put on their oxygen masks and to breathe into their lives the living presence of an awesome God. By doing so, they just might rediscover authentic and effective ministry.

– Bill Easum, _Put on your own oxygen mask first_, pp. 27-29

Keep a firm grasp on both your character and your teaching. Don't be diverted. Just keep at it. Both you and those who hear you will experience salvation.
    – _1 Timothy 4:16 (The Message)_

EXERCISE

Pastors often set goals based on advancing their ministry at the neglect of their personal growth. Sit down and set personal long term and short term goals.

Journal

44

Preacher Heal Thyself

The preacher's sharpest and strongest preaching should be to himself. His most difficult, delicate, laborious, and thorough work must be with himself.... It is not great talents nor great learning nor great preachers that God needs, but men great and holiness, great in faith, great in love, great infidelity, great for God – men always preaching by holy sermons in the pulpit, by holy lives out of it. These can mold a generation for God.

After this order, the early Christians were formed. Men they were of solid mold, preachers after the heavenly type – heroic, stalwart, soldierly, saintly. Preaching with them in self-denying, self crucifying, serious, toilsome, mortar business. They apply themselves to it in a way that pulled on a generation, and four minutes when the generation yet unborn for God...

The real sermon is made in the closet. The man – God's man – is made in the closet. His life and his profoundest convictions were born in his secret communion with God. The burdened and tearful agony of his spirit, his weightiest and sweetest messages were got one alone with God. Prayer makes the man; prayer makes the preacher; prayer makes the pastor.

– EM Bounds, *Preacher and Prayer*, pp. 5-13

And this I pray, that your love may abound still more and more in knowledge and all discernment, that you may approve the things that are excellent, that you may be sincere and without offense till the day of Christ, being filled with the fruits of righteousness which are by Jesus Christ, to the glory and praise of God.
–Philippians 1:9-11 (NKJV)

EXERCISE

Accountability has been called "sharing the necessary information before its necessary". Find someone out of your immediate circle of influence to be an accountability partner on a regular basis.

*"As fishers of men remember there are no small fish
or big fish in God's eyes- just fish!"*

– *Rich Earl*

Journal

45

Toiling in Obscurity

Why does God test those he calls with a time of obscurity before he entrusts them with their missions? Could it be that he desires relationship before service? If we were to get our commission right from the start, we'd never have time to get to know God as a person, would we? We'd be busy working...

Relish the time of obscurity. You may wish for them when you've been commissioned and the busy days come.

Be flattered if God "puts you on the shelf" for awhile. He just wants to get to know you as you before he knows you as his worker. You the person, with your fancies and foibles, with your delights and dislikes.

God seems to love obscure pastors. After all, there are so many of us! Like most pastors, we don't have "big names," aren't famous, and are in no danger of becoming so. This is quite in keeping with the way God loves to operate, employing ordinary people, the weak, the foolish, the obscure—as vessels and channels of His blessing to men. Finding joy in our seeming obscurity is a secret storehouse few enjoy.

Indeed, obscurity in ministry has its challenges. There is generally a lack of resources- talent, money, personnel. There are traditions we may neither understand nor agree with. There is often a lack of vision as the people see no point in dreaming as they are content where they are.

The pastor in obscurity is also at risk of depression as results and affirmation can be hard to come by. Similarly, there are many temptations which we must be on guard against. It is easy to take on a dictatorial stance as there may be few whom we can share the leadership load with. We can often fall into the habit of laziness because of the lack of accountability. Then there is the tendency to envy larger churches with more influence and resources, or to imagine they must be using methods filled with compromise to fill their pews.

Finally, there are great benefits in ministry in an obscure place. The sense of community is generally stronger and more organic. It can be easy to observe real visible change not only in the church, but in the community in a small amount of time. We also enjoy greater accessibility to public officials, local media, the business community and school systems. There is also freedom to experiment- lower cost and risk.

– Richard Earl

Do everything readily and cheerfully—no bickering, no second-guessing allowed! Go out into the world uncorrupted, a breath of fresh air in this squalid and polluted society. Provide people with a glimpse of good living and of the living God. Carry the light-giving Message into the night so I'll have good cause to be proud of you on the day that Christ returns. You'll be living proof that I didn't go to all this work for nothing. Even if I am executed here and now, I'll rejoice in being an element in the offering of your faith that you make on Christ's altar, a part of your rejoicing. But turnabout's fair play—you must join me in my rejoicing. Whatever you do, don't feel sorry for me.

–Philippians 2:14-18 (The Message)

EXERCISE

Visit a small local church on your vacation. Enter into worship as a participant. Neglect to share your position. Listen to the message with fresh ears. Write the pastor a note of encouragement.

Journal

46

Extruded to Higher Places

Jesus commands Christians to seek consciously the lowest position. All of us — pastors, teachers... are tempted to say, I will take the larger place because it will give me more influence for Jesus Christ. Both individual Christians and Christian organizations fall prey to the temptation of rationalizing this away as we build bigger and bigger empires. According to the Scripture, this is backward: we should consciously take the lowest place unless the Lord himself extrudes us into a greater one.

The word extrude is important here. To be extruded is to be forced out under pressure into a desired shape. Picture a huge press jamming soft metal at high pressure through a die, so that the metal comes out in a certain shape. This is the way of the Christian: he should choose the lesser place until God extrudes him into a position of more responsibility and authority.

Let me suggest to reasons why we ought not grasp the larger place. First, we should seek the lowest place because there it is easier to be quiet before the face of the Lord. I did not say easy; in no place, no matter how small or humble, is it easy to be quiet before God. But it is certainly easier in some places than others. And the little places, where I can more easily be close to God, should be my preference. I'm not saying that it is impossible to be quiet before God in a greater place, but God must be allowed to choose when a Christian is ready to be extruded into such a place, for only He knows when a person will be able to have some quietness before him in the midst of increased pressure and responsibility.

Quietness and peace before God are more important than any influence a position may seem to give, for we must stay in step with God to have the power of the Holy Spirit. If by taking a bigger place our quietness with God is lost, then to that extent our fellowship with him is broken and we are living in the flesh, and the final result will not be as great, no matter how important the larger place may look in the eyes of other men or in our own eyes. Always there will be a battle, always we will be less than perfect, but if the place is too big and too active for our present spiritual condition, then it is too big.

One of the loveliest incidents in the early church occurred when Barnabas concluded that Paul was the man of the hour and then had to seek him out because Paul had gone back to Tarsus, his own little place. Paul was not up there nominating himself; he was back in Tarsus, even out of communication as far as we can tell. When Paul called himself "the chief of sinners... not meet to be an apostle" (1 Tim. 1:15, 1 Corinthians 15:9), he was not speaking just for outward form sake. From what he said elsewhere and from his actions, we can see that this was Paul's mentality. Paul, the man of leadership for the whole Gentile world, was perfectly willing to be in Tarsus until God said to him, "this is the moment."

– Francis Schaeffer, from The Complete Works of Francis Schaeffer, pp. 5-14

Now he told a parable to those who were invited, when he noticed how they chose the places of honor, saying to them, "When you are invited by someone to a wedding feast, do not sit down in a place of honor, lest someone more distinguished than you be invited by him, and he who invited you both will come and say to you, 'Give your place to this person,' and then you will begin with shame to take the lowest place. But when you are invited, go and sit in the lowest place, so that when your host comes he may say to you, 'Friend, move up higher.' Then you will be honored in the presence of all who sit at table with you. For everyone who exalts himself will be humbled, and he who humbles himself will be exalted."

–Luke 14:7-11 (ESV)

EXERCISE

Make an effort to step back this week and allow someone else to lead, take credit or receive praise. Deliberately defer praise of any kind and wait for God to lift you up in His own time.

*"Our ways don't become His ways until
we are undone..."*

— *Terry Taylor*

Journal

47

What We Expect from Preaching

In a certain sense every young minister is conceited. He begins his Ministry in a conceited condition. At least every man begins with extravagant expectations of what his Ministry is to result in. We come out from it by and by. A man's first wonder when he begins to preach is that people do not come to hear him. After a while, if he is good for anything, he begins to wonder that they do. He finds out that the old Adam is too strong for the young Melanchthon. It is not strange that it should be so.

The student for the Ministry has to a large extent comprehended the force by which he is to work, but he has not measured the resistance that he is to meet. He knows the power of the truth of which he is all full, but he has not estimated the sin of which the world is all full. The more earnest and intense and full of love for God and man he is, the more impossible does it seem that he should not do great things for his master. And then the character of the ministries, it seems to me, depends very largely upon the ways in which they passed out of that first self-confidence and upon what conditions come afterwards, when it is gone.

– Quoting Phillips Brooks, from *A Ministers Obstacles*, by Ralph Turnbull, p 153

So when they had appointed him a day, many came to him at his lodging, to whom he explained and solemnly testified of the kingdom of God, persuading them concerning Jesus from both the Law of Moses and the Prophets, from morning till evening.
–Acts 28:23 (NKJV)

EXERCISE

Take an older minister to lunch and ask him what he has learned since he was your age.

"Preach the gospel, die and be forgotten."

— Count Zinzendorf

Journal

48

Subversives

Pastors occupy an odd niche in American culture. Christian communities employ us to lead worship, teach and preach the Scriptures, and provide guidance and encouragement in the pilgrim way. Within our congregation, we experience a modest honor in our position.

Occasionally one of us rises to national prominence and catches the attention of large numbers of people with the charisma of sunny, millennial cheerleading or (less often) the scary forecasts of Armageddon. But most of us are known by name only to or congregations and, except for ceremonial appearances at weddings, funerals, and bull roasts, are not in the public eye.

In general, people treat us with respect, we are not considered important in any social, cultural, or economic way. In parody we are usually treated as harmless in a sense, in satire as shiftless parasites.

This is not what most of us had in mind when we signed on. We had not counted on anything either so benign or so marginal. The images forming our pastoral expectations had a good deal more fierceness to them: Moses bearding the pharaoh; Jeremiah with fire in his mouth; Peter swashbucklingly reckless as the lead apostle; Paul's careering through prison and ecstasy, shipwreck and kerygma. The kingdom of God in which we had apprenticed ourselves was presented to us as revolutionary, a dangerously unwelcome intruder in the old boy club of thrones, dominions, principalities and powers.

The vocabulary we learned in preparation for our work was the language of battle ("we fight not against flesh and blood"), danger ("your adversary the devil prowls around like a roaring lion, seeking someone to devour"), and austerity ("take up your cross and follow me"). After arriving on the job, we find precious few opportunities to use our leadership language. And so, like the two years of Spanish we took in high school, it is so nonfunctional from nonuse.

Did we learn the wrong language? Did we acquire the wrong images? Did we apprentice ourselves to the wrong master?

Everybody treats us so nicely no one seems to think we mean what we say. When we say "kingdom of God," no one gets apprehensive, as if we had just announced (which we thought we had) that a powerful army is poised on the border, ready to invade. When we say radical things like "Christ", "love, "believe", "peace", and "sin" words that in other times and cultures excited martyrdoms – the sounds enter the stream of conversation with no more splash than baseball scores and grocery prices.

It's hard to maintain a self-concept as a revolutionary when everyone treats us with the same affability they give the grocer.

Are these people right? Is their way of life in no danger from us? Is what we say about God and his ways among us not real in the same way that Chevrolets and basketball teams and fresh garden spinach are real? Many pastors, realizing the opinion polls overwhelmingly repudiate their self-concept, submit to the cultural verdict and slip into the role of chaplain to the culture. It is easy to do. But some pastors do not; they become subversives in the culture.

– Eugene Peterson, *The Contemplative Pastor*, pp 38 - 40

Therefore, brethren, be even more diligent to make your call and election sure, for if you do these things you will never stumble; for so an entrance will be supplied to you abundantly into the everlasting kingdom of our Lord and Savior Jesus Christ.
– 2 Peter 1:10-12 (KJV)

EXERCISE

Perform an unseen task today. Find a way to profoundly bless someone who would never expect it, and who will not know the origin of the blessing. Be deliberate and do not tell a soul.

*"79% of all Yale ministry graduates
from 1702-1779 served one
congregation all their lives."*
                                    —Leonard Sweet

Journal

49

Conflict and Intimacy

I heard Nancy Ortberg say something that bothered me at the time. "Conflict is the only way to intimacy," she said. I was intrigued by it, and for me it has come to embody a hidden secret of ministry.

I am not drawn to categorical statements like this one. I tend to see things in shades of gray rather than black and white. "Conflict can't be the only way to intimacy," I thought, there must be some other paths.

The first and most obvious reality here is that the determinate conflict of the cross produced the ultimate opportunity for intimacy for the entire human race- for any who will respond. The battle raged in the twisted and bloodied body of the Savior and broke a course for us to enjoy the real and awesome, intimate and personal presence of the Father.

Likewise, a birthing mother emerges from the

grueling battle to tenderly embrace the little one in the ultimate act of intimacy. Without her struggle there would be stillbirth. Her conflict forces life out of her and into the child. We pray for her in the struggle, and celebrate with her in motherhood.

I am testing this truth in other places too. I do so anticipating the tender quiet walks in the warming spring air that will inevitably be possible on the other side. The conflict helps me appreciate the peace and growth that will surely come.

Our church is located in an old coal mining culture that has made an art out of conflict. Our church family has been through some major battles in the past 25 years, and some casualties have fallen. Having weathered some conflicts here myself I have wondered if anything good can ever come from the splits and quarrels that have sometimes divided us. Now I have hope that we can transition into a culture of peace and close relationship, modeled by our leadership, if we will learn to allow the conflict to create intimacy.

– Richard Earl with thanks to Nancy Ortberg

Now Jacob lifted his eyes and looked, and there, Esau
was coming, and with him were four hundred men....
Then he crossed over before them and bowed himself to
the ground seven times, until he came near to his
brother. But Esau ran to meet him, and embraced him,
and fell on his neck and kissed him, and they wept.
– Genesis 33:1-4 (NKJV)

EXERCISE

Write a letter of appreciation or encouragement
to someone every day this week.

Journal

50

Prayer and Pulpit

Go from your knees to the chapel. Get a renewal of your commission every time you go to preach in a renewed sense of the favor of God. Carry your authority to declare the gospel of Christ not in your hand but in your heart. ...

Never assume an air of importance while in the pulpit. You stand in an awful place and God hates the proud man... Self-confidence will soon lead to a forgetfulness of the presence of God. Then you will speak your own words and perhaps in your own spirit, too.

The pulpit appears to me analogous to the box in which the witnesses are sworn in a court of justice, "to say the truth, the whole truth, and nothing but the truth." You are a witness for God and are bound by more, if possible, than an oath to speak the truth in righteousness and love and to declare faithfully and solemnly, according to the best of your knowledge, the whole counsel of God. You should never come into the congregation but in the spirit of prayer. Let your mind be wound up into that spirit in your closet; and then, in your prayers in the congregation, you'll appear what you should be – a man familiar with God. Examine the Scriptures and you will find that all the holy men of God prayed in this way: they came directly to the throne... Ever considering themselves in the presence of God, the very commencement of their supplication seems no other than an external continuance of prayers in which their hearts had been long previously engaged.

... while you are engaged in the pulpit in recommending the salvation of God, endeavor to feel the truth you preach and diffuse a divine animation through every part. As the preacher appears to preach, the people here and believe. You may set it down as an incontrovertible truth that none of your hearers will be more effective with your discourse than yourself. A dull, dead preacher makes a dull dead congregation.

– Refiners Fire vol. 1, Adam Clarke *Letter to a Preacher*, pp 114 – 115

And it came to pass, when Moses entered the tabernacle, that the pillar of cloud descended and stood at the door of the tabernacle, and the Lord talked with Moses. All the people saw the pillar of cloud standing at the tabernacle door, and all the people rose and worshiped, each man in his tent door.

So the Lord spoke to Moses face to face, as a man
speaks to his friend. And he would return to the camp,
but his servant Joshua the son of Nun, a young man,
did not depart from the tabernacle.

−Exodus 33:9-11 (NKJV)

EXERCISE

This week spend as much time in prayer as in study. Look for new places and opportunities for prayer in preparing your heart to speak for God.

Journal

51

Bitzer was a Banker

In 1982, Baker Book House reissued a 1969 book of daily scripture readings in Hebrew and Greek called Light on the Path. The readings were short, and vocabulary helps were given with the Hebrew verses. The aim of the editor, who died in 1980, was to help pastors preserve and improve their ability to interpret the Bible from the original languages.

His name was Heinrich Bitzer. He was a banker.

I have a debt to pay to Heinrich Bitzer, and I would like to discharge it by exhorting all of us to ponder his thesis: "The more a theologian detaches himself from the basic Hebrew and Greek text of Holy Scripture, the more he detaches himself from the source of real theology! And real theology is the foundation of a fruitful and blessed ministry."

One of the greatest tragedies in the church today is the depreciation of the pastoral office. From seminaries to denominational headquarters, the prevalent mood and theme is managerial, organizational, and psychological. And we think thereby to heighten our professional self-esteem!...

We need to recover our vision of the pastoral office- which embraces, if nothing else, the passion and power to understand the original revelation of God. We need to pray for the day when pastors can carry their Greek Testaments to conferences and seminars without being greeted with one liners- the day when the esteem of God's Word and it's careful exposition is so high among pastors those that do not have the skill will humbly bless and encourage those who do and will encourage younger men to get what they never got. Oh, for the day when prayer and grammar will meet each other with great spiritual combustion!

It is never too late to learn the languages. There are men who began after retirement! It is not a question of time, but of values. John Newton, the author of Amazing Grace and former sea captain, was a pastor's pastor with a winsome, gentle love for people who, nevertheless, thought it important to pursue the languages. He once counseled a young minister, "The original scriptures well deserve your pains, and will richly repay them."

– John Piper, *Brothers we are not professionals*, pp. 82-85

Bring the cloak that I left with Carpus at Troas when
you come--and the books, especially the parchments.
— 2 Timothy 4:13 (NKJV)

EXERCISE

Call up an old mentor, teacher or pastoral colleague and take them to lunch or send them a note or a gift to say thank you.

Journal

52

Sentry for a Snowdrop

With every generation new conditions present themselves to the church. Society, business, politics, home, and everything has undergone a marked change within the last quarter of a century. The church has lost her grip upon these times if she does not move with them, and the men of this generation pass by without ever a thought of crossing its threshold. We must change our thought and work and machinery, and even the course of the ship, if we are to fulfill our mission.

The old truth is sacred; old methods may not be. Truth cannot be changed; methods must always be changing. He who is wide awake, and lives in his own time, and pushes to the front, and devises new methods, will be the center of gravity of the men of the world. He who runs in old ruts, and preaches old sermons, and works with old plans, is dead as far as the world is concerned. He has neither life nor power, and that is death. He who studies the right way of presenting truth, and the art of putting things, and the skill in catching men, and understands the importance of tact and sanctified common sense, is "like a tree planted by the rivers of water, that brings forth his fruit in his season. His leaf also shall not wither, and whatsoever he doeth shall prosper."

If the old methods are worn out and ineffective, it is folly and sin to continue their operation. The emperor of Russia, while showing a distinguished visitor over his palace, was asked by the latter why a sentinel was placed on a small grass plot in the grounds. The emperor called his aide-de-camp and asked for information. This the latter was unable to give. The officer for the day was sent for, but he, too, was unable to enlighten the czar. "Send me the general in command of the forces here," said the emperor. The general came, but could give no further information than that his orders were to post an armed sentinel on that spot. "Investigate it, then," said the czar shortly, "and report the result to me." A long search in the military order-book revealed the fact that, eighty years ago, Catherine II, looking from a window in her apartment, had seen the first spring flower shoot up above the snow. She ordered a sentinel to be placed in order to prevent anyone from breaking the snowdrop. No one thought to countermand the order afterward, and so for eighty years a sentinel had kept watch on that very spot; a human monument of blind, useless obedience to old orders and customs. Many a preacher stands within the courts of the church a sentinel over some withered flower of the past.

That same czar, while going through his palace one day, noticed some repairs were being made, and, wishing to make inquiry, he beckoned to a workman nearby, who immediately dropped his tools and approached the emperor. Before the latter could speak to him a rifle shot rang out, and the man fell dead. A hidden sentinel had not seen the emperor beckon, and, in accordance with orders to shoot anyone coming unsummoned within twenty paces of the czar, he had killed the workman, whom he had suspected of approaching the emperor for the purpose of murdering him.

The man who is doing some new work in the kingdom of God, and reaching the churchless and Christless men, is beckoned to the side of his Master to receive commendation, while the impulsive and shortsighted guard over antiquities tries to shoot him down.

The church for the times must meet the church of the times. It must be of the Columbus spirit, and, with consecrated determination, discover the new world. It will find the discord in the music of modern life, and bring it back to key note and harmony. It will brave any storm, and sail any sea to reach the great continent of man's needs, and to satisfy the longings of his heart.

– Cortland Myers, *Why Men do not go to church*, pp. 13-19

Then the scribes and Pharisees who were from Jerusalem came to Jesus, saying, "Why do Your disciples transgress the tradition of the elders? For they do not wash their hands when they eat bread."
He answered and said to them, "Why do you also transgress the commandment of God because of your tradition?
…Thus you have made the commandment of God of no effect by your tradition. Hypocrites! Well did Isaiah prophesy about you, saying: 'These people draw near to Me with their mouth, And honor Me with their lips, But their heart is far from Me. And in vain they worship Me, Teaching as doctrines the commandments of men.'"

– Matthew 15:1-9 (NKJV)

EXERCISE

Take a walk or hike through a local park in total silence. Listen only for God's still small voice.

"To reach people no one else is reaching, we have to be willing to do things no one else is doing."
– Craig Groeschel

Journal

Bibliography

Baxter, Richard (1885). The Reformed Pastor, New York, American Tract Society

Bounds, EM Preacher and Prayer, Grand Rapids, Zondervan

Bunyan, John (1998) The Pilgrim's Progress in Modern English, N. Brunswick, NJ, Bridge-Logos

Chambers, Oswald (1965) Workmen of God London, Oswald Chambers Pub Assoc.

Chambers, Oswald (1958) Called of God, Kent, Great Britain, Oswald Chambers Publications

Chapman, J. Wilbur (1918) The Minister's Handicap, New York, American Tract Society

Cuyler, Theodore (1893) The Young Preacher New York, Revell

Gee, Donald (1952) Concerning Shepherds and Sheepfolds, London, Elim

Gurnall, William (1989) The Christian in Complete Armour, Chicago, Moody Press

Jefferson, Charles (1901) Quiet Hints to Growing Preachers, New York, Crowell

Jefferson, Charles (1912)The Minister as Shepherd, New York, Crowell

Keller, Phillip (1978) A Shepherd Looks at the Good Shepherd, Grand Rapids, Zondervan

MacDonald, George (1888). God's Word to His Children, New York, Funk and Wagnall's

McNeal, Reggie (2006) Practicing Greatness, San Francisco, Jossey- Bass

Murray, Andrew (1895) With Christ, New York, Bay View

Murray, Andrew (1897) Waiting on God, New York, Revell

Myers, Cortland (1899) Why men do not go to church, New York, Funk and Wagnall's

Peterson, Eugene (1993) Working the Angles, Grand Rapids, Eerdman's

Peterson, Eugene (1989) The Contemplative Pastor, Grand Rapids, Eerdman's

Peterson, Robert L. & Strauch, Alexander (1991), Agape Leadership, Littleton, Colo, Lewis & Roth

Ravenhill, Leonard (1963) Meat for Men, Minneapolis, Bethany

Sanders, Oswald J. (2007) Spiritual Leadership, Chicago, Moody

Schaeffer, Francis, (1998) The Complete Works of Francis Schaeffer, Crossway pp 5-14

Slemming, CW (1949) Echoes from the Hills of Bethlehem, London, Henry Walter

Spurgeon, Charles Lectures to my Students, Lynchburg, Va, Old-Time Gospel Hour

Wilkerson, David (1984). Refiner's Fire Journal,
    Lindale, Tx. World Challenge
Willard, Dallas (1988) The Spirit of the Disciplines,
    San Francisco, Harper and Row

Many thanks for the following permissions:

CPSIA information can be obtained
at www.ICGtesting.com
Printed in the USA
LVHW090926281018
595117LV00039B/2109/P